Leave The Corporate World Behind

Leave The Corporate World Behind

By Adrienne Dupree

Copyright © 2014 by Adrienne Dupree
ISBN: 978-1-937988-13-5

Hunter's Moon Publishing
http://HuntersMoonPublishing.com

Cover design by Shawn Hansen

Dedication

This book is dedicated to my mother, Whyethia Barbara Johnson Knight from whom I inherited my entrepreneurial spirit. She moved from the corporate world to the entrepreneurial world several times in her lifetime. Her example gave me the courage to follow my dreams when I decided I wanted to leave the corporate world behind. Even though she is not physically here to see me make this transformation, I know she is looking down from heaven cheering me on.

Table of Contents

Introduction

Welcome to Leave The Corporate World Behind. Are you in corporate America and are tired of the rat race? Are you looking to do something different? Are you tired of office politics and the countless hours of uncompensated overtime? Even if you feel like you are trapped, I want you to know that there is a way to get out.

This book is all about people who used to work in corporate America who now have an online marketing business. It is also about people who are still working in corporate America but have a part-time online marketing business. The book tells their story of why they decided to get out of corporate America, what you need to do to prepare to leave, their biggest obstacles as well as advice you can follow on your journey.

The journeys that you read about are very inspirational and motivational. Once you read this book, you will know that you have what it takes to fulfill your dreams and start on the path to entrepreneurship.

Foreword
by Connie Ragen Green

I don't remember exactly when I met Adrienne Dupree, but it must have been right around the time we both attended a marketing event in Atlanta several years ago. I was struck by how she spoke and carried herself, and knew immediately this was one very smart and extremely nice person I wanted to get to know better. I identified her as a fellow introvert, even though I can be loud and outgoing at times, at least in short spurts. When Adrienne finally laughed out loud at one of my jokes I felt that we had made a connection that would take our friendship to the next level and beyond.

Adrienne has a background very different from my own; she has been a part of the corporate world all of her adult working life. I admire what she has been able to accomplish in that space, as I know it can be intensely competitive and challenging. Although she has been very successful in the corporate arena, at some point she decided that it was a part of her life she would be willing to leave behind when she could replace her income with work she would do exclusively online.

She asked me to tell you a little bit about myself here, so here goes.

After college and throughout my twenties I went from job to job, never quite fitting in or feeling like anything was right for me. I finally decided to get my real estate license and did enjoy that to some extent. Soon I began to feel as though my life would never have true meaning, and I sought out careers in banking, insurance, and more. I continued to work in real estate during this time as a way to earn income, but my heart truly wasn't in it each day.

One day I had just come into the office when I saw a group sitting in front of a small television set in the back. I had completely forgotten that it was the day when the United States was launching another space shuttle into orbit and sat down to experience it with the others. It was January 28, 1986, and on this day the Space Shuttle Challenger broke apart just seventy-three seconds into the flight. All seven crew members were killed, including Christa McAuliffe, the first teacher chosen to go into space.

I watched in shock as they showed her husband, parents, and two young children realizing what had happened, and then flashed to her school in New Hampshire where hundreds of students were watching on television. In that moment I made the decision to fulfill a long time dream of becoming a classroom teacher, and within one year I had earned a preliminary credential and was teaching in my own classroom.

For the next twenty years I worked as a classroom teacher by day, and continued with real estate after school, on weekends, and during school vacations. For the first ten years this worked out well, but after going through cancer and having a serious work injury it began to wear me out. The school system in Los Angeles also changed drastically during this time, finally making my teaching seem like a job I no longer wanted to participate in. I made the decision to find another way to earn a living, and in 2006 I resigned from the school district at the end of the school year and gave away my best real estate clients. I knew I was burning my bridges and believed this was the best thing for my future. The rest, as they say, is history.

So even though Adrienne and I come from very different backgrounds, I believe we are kindred spirits in our mutual desire to own our time and financial future. This type of freedom is worth every moment we put into it, as it allows us to explore the world with childlike eyes and discover just why we are here on earth for our journey. This may sound quite esoteric, but I honestly believe it is important to know who we are as human beings, on a deep and spiritual level before we can truly achieve success in the outside world.

It's a bold move to tell yourself and then the world that you are ready to leave a career behind once and for all that was more than twenty years in the making. When Adrienne first told me this was her intention I questioned her motives. To those of us on the outside, a well-paying corporate job doing something you enjoy and are good at appears to be an excellent opportunity. Upon closer examination I discovered that Adrienne's and my experiences in the workplace were actually quite similar. I agreed to help her move forward with her plan to build a lucrative business online that would allow her to finally leave the corporate world behind once and for all.

Over these past few years I have watched Adrienne struggle to get started, take massive action with the tasks and activities I have challenged her with, and move forward in a way that is sure to get massive results. Her efforts have been impressive, and each project she commits to brings her closer to her goals. We have partnered in a joint venture for one product, and now she is off and running as she creates new information products each month and becomes more adept with affiliate marketing. Writing this book is just another example of how she jumps in to turn her dreams into reality.

When I think of Adrienne I have to smile with joy and pride. I'm reminded of the opening lines of a popular song which goes like this:

"Once in your lifetime you find her
Someone that turns your life around"

I honestly believe we have only seen the tip of the iceberg with what this savvy entrepreneur will be able to achieve as an online entrepreneur in the coming years. When Adrienne finally comes in to her own with products and courses and books and speaking presentations she will be a force to be reckoned with. For me as her mentor it's like watching a gifted and talented child find their voice and step forward into the limelight.

I have encouraged her to surround herself with other successful people who are making things happen for themselves and their businesses, and to steer clear of those who are stagnating by doing the same things they did last year and the year before. With her big heart it is natural for her to want to pull those people along with her, but this type of action quickly becomes an albatross around your neck. Instead, I've asked her to connect with those entrepreneurs she meets who have big ideas and take massive actions who are also willing to 'do for a year what others won't in order to live the way others can't, forever'.

Adrienne is a rare gem and a gift from God and I count my blessings to have her in my life. She recently came to Santa Barbara to attend my Mastermind Retreat and it was obvious to me and to the others how smart and intuitive she is when it comes to her business acumen and in her life choices. I believe that she saw herself differently after our week together and will now settle for nothing short of great success. She also has a strong sense of family, faith, and community, and is quick to share her joys, as well as her obstacles with those she meets. I love learning more about her son, her beloved women's basketball team, and her love of warm weather and the beach. If only we could all be so well-rounded.

Thank you, Adrienne, for everything you have given me in the way of friendship and business ideas over these past few years, as I truly treasure our relationship. And may we have many more years together to learn and grow and continue to create the lives we were destined to live.

Connie Ragen Green
Santa Barbara, California
February, 2014
http://ConnieRagenGreen.com

Leave the Corporate World Behind: Software Engineer to Online Marketer
by Adrienne Dupree

From Lawyer to Engineer

I grew up in the Washington, DC area and attended Eleanor Roosevelt High School in Greenbelt, MD. I was part of the Science & Technology program which required you to pass a test in order to participate in this program. This was a 4 year program which was unique. At that time, junior high was from 7th grade to 9th grade and high school started in 10th grade. The Science & Technology program started in 9th grade and it was a county wide program with students attending from all over Prince Georges County, Maryland. I took a ton of science and math classes during high school and even had to do a year-long research project. By the time I finished high school, I had college credits in Spanish, Biology and Chemistry but was a little burned out. When it was time to go to college, I had decided that I didn't want anything else to do with all that

Math and Science and decided to major in Political Science in preparation for a career as a lawyer.

I was accepted to Boston University but my family did not have the finances for me to attend. I was also accepted to Towson University which was a state school. Unfortunately, they ran out of housing so I could not attend there either. I ended up attending Bowie State University which is also a state school. I started there as a Political Science major. Since I did not have a technical major, I was enrolled in a general math class. Quickly, my math teacher, Dr. Johnny Ponds, realized I was in the wrong math class and moved me to a higher level class. That class was not challenging enough either so Dr. Ponds just gave me my own work. He was the one that was instrumental in me changing my major.

I really didn't like Political Science. I found it very boring and not satisfying at all. Dr. Ponds encouraged me to explore the Dual Degree Engineering program. Ultimately, I changed my major. The Dual Degree Engineering program was a 5 year program. You attended school for 5 years and ended up with 2 degrees from 2 different schools. I attended Bowie for 3 years to pursue a Mathematics degree. I was really a year behind because my major was Political Science as a freshman. I took 21 credits a semester to catch up so I could finish my Math degree in 3 years. After that, I attended George Washington University for 2 years for my Electrical Engineering degree with a Computer Engineering concentration. After 5 years, I ended up with 2 degrees and graduated from both schools in May 1986. The graduations were one week apart. My resume looks pretty odd because I list 2 degrees from 2 different schools with the same graduation year. I have had to explain this on more than one occasion. Even though I did not attend my first choice for college, I believe that it was meant for me to attend Bowie State University.

One year after I graduated, I decided to go back to school and pursue a Master's degree. At this time, I was working full time, so I attended graduate school part-time. I graduated with a Masters in Computer Science with a concentration in Artificial Intelligence from George Washington University.

Even though I am a pretty serious person, I do have fun and have a few hobbies. I like playing golf; reading; attending concerts, theatre and cultural events; jazz clubs; travel and attending basketball games. I love beaches especially the ones in the Caribbean. There is something about warm clear water.

My biggest passion is women's basketball. I have season tickets to the Washington Mystics which is a WNBA team. I also have season tickets to the University of Maryland Women's Basketball Team. I also attend the ACC tournament, the CAA tournament, NCAA tournament games and any other games that I can fit in. I have been known to leave my house after work on a week day to drive 4 or 5 hours to North Carolina, attend a basketball game, drive back home in the middle of the night and go to work the next day. I know this may sound crazy to you, but I love it. As they say, "All work and no play makes Jane a dull girl".

My Corporate Life Journey

When I graduated from college, I started my career as a Software Engineer. My last two years of college, I worked part-time as a Software Engineer in corporate America so I already had some experience. The company that I worked for during college actually offered me I job, but I turned it down because I got offers for more money. I was also offered a job with the Naval Research Lab that I also turned down. In hindsight, if I had taken that government job, I could have potentially retired in a few years. I stayed at my first job for about a year and moved to another company.

I went to another defense company and stayed there for 4 years. It was a wonderful company. They paid for me to get my Master's degree up front which is pretty rare. They also had very good benefits including sick leave and an 8% 401K match. I left there because I wanted to use my Master's Degree which had a concentration in Artificial Intelligence. I probably should have been a little more patient and stuck it out. When you are young, you don't necessarily think about 401K matching and things like that.

I went on to my third company and stayed there for approximately 7 years. It was a big defense contractor. I loved my job and even had a chance to go to Brussels for two weeks since I was working on a NATO contract. I loved my career and moved up pretty quickly to a Software Lead where I was managing other people. At some point in your career, you have to decide if you want to stay technical or go into management. I decided that I wanted to go into Management so my career took another turn. The only reason I left this job was because my contract ended and I was left with a long commute to Reston, Virginia.

My next job was perfect. It was 5 minutes from my house, and the work was very interesting. I held jobs as a Software Lead, Software Development Manager, Project Manager, Deputy Program Manager and a Program Manager. I worked on a NASA contract for about 7 years. I also worked on other contracts for NOAA, United States Patent & Trade Office and the FBI. Things were great until about 2 years before I left.

I have always worked as a government contractor with big companies which is pretty normal in the Washington, DC area. These companies are known as "Beltway Bandits". In November 2012, that all changed. I left the job that I had for 16.5 years and started working as a Program Manager for a small company. This was a huge change for me, but this is what I needed to move me to my ultimate goal of being a full-time online marketer. I currently work from home which is preparing me for my exodus from corporate America. I now know that I am disciplined enough to work without being in an office full of people with my boss being able to see what I am doing.

My Corporate America Exodus

A lot of people are puzzled when they find out that I want to leave the corporate world behind. Why would you do that Adrienne? You not only have a job, but a successful career. Well, there were many things that happened over the years that made me second guess my career in corporate America. Over the years, the expectations changed and I found myself working 60+ hours a week. This led to me neglecting many things in my life to include my family, house, car, friends, finances and health. Dealing with a lot of stress and working a lot of hours definitely takes a toll on you.

The climate at my previous job changed and all of a sudden, there was so much politics and doing a good job was not good enough anymore. Because I was not willing to say what people wanted to hear, I found myself being punished. It is amazing that people would rather hear a good story than the truth. I had always received very good performance reviews and all of a sudden I was a "Needs Improvement" employee. This resulted in my being put on a Performance Improvement Plan and not receiving a pay raise for the year. As someone who is an over-achiever; this really affected my confidence and self-esteem. I started to believe the things that were said about me.

When our contract came up for renewal, my job was posted with a lower grade. I was then asked why I did not apply for the job. To me this was ludicrous. First of all, I was already doing the job and why would I apply for a job that was a lower grade than the job I was already doing. I am not into playing games and I guess I am not really cut out for "office politics". Ultimately, I got my job back without having to take a pay cut. After all of this, I was still trying to stick it out because I had severance and a pension. If I was laid off, then I would get one week of pay for every year of service.

When our contract was finally renewed, things really changed. Our benefits were changed. I no longer had severance, profit sharing or a pension. Also, I lost 2 holidays. At this point, it was no incentive to stay at this company. I still had the pension that had been accumulating over the last 16.5 years, but there would be no more contributions to it. I now felt the 16.5 years of sacrifice meant nothing. Maybe these changes were what I needed to finally have the courage to leave.

Before our contract was renewed, there was a gap in the contracts. I was closing out the old contract so I was able to still work. Many of my employees really suffered during this time. People were forced to exhaust their vacation and then take up to two weeks of leave without pay. I have always been the type of manager that really looks out for my employees, but this was completely out of my control.

The contract was finally awarded and people came back to work. The dollar amount of the contract had been cut, so then I was told that there would not be funding for me. Because of this, I was forced to take 5 weeks of vacation. Thank God, I had the vacation to take. Otherwise, I would have had to take leave without pay as well. There were a lot of things that fell through the cracks while I was gone. Even though I was the Software Development Manager, I performed a lot of other duties as well. I was brought back to work but ultimately, I was given a layoff notice. The layoff notice was rescinded but at that point, I was done. I stepped up my job search activities.

The last straw was we were moved from offices and cubicles to a conference room. It was awful. We were stacked on top of each other because of the way the contract was bid. There was no money for people to have offices or cubicles anymore. Fortunately for me, this happened as I was leaving so I was only there for less than a week. It was so crowded in there that every time I backed my chair up, I would bump into the chair of one of my coworkers.

My new job is completely different and I am appreciated again. It is a small company that is very "employee friendly". This is a much better situation for me. I don't work as many hours so I am able to work on my business in the evenings and the weekends. Even though the conditions are 100%

better at my new job, I have already decided that I am ready to do something different in my life.

Preparation for Leaving Corporate America

Once you decide to leave Corporate America, you need to come up with a plan. I don't suggest you just quit your job without really being prepared. The first thing you need to determine is whether you are disciplined enough to work for yourself without a boss. You have to be self-motivated to be your own boss. There is no one telling what to do and giving you deadlines. Also you need to ask yourself, can you work from home without someone looking over your shoulder to make sure you are really working?

Before you leave your job, you should start your online marketing business on a part-time basis. This gives you a chance to determine your niche and actually get started. You want to have some momentum before you leave your job. Not only will you gain great experience but you also have the monetary resources necessary for your start-up expenses.

In order to really be successful at starting your online marketing business on a part-time business, you will have to make some sacrifices. Look for things that you can cut out of your life so you will have time in the evenings and weekends to work on your business. The one thing I did right away was drastically reduce the amount of television that I watched. For the programs that I did not want to give up, I now tape them so I can skip the commercials. I also go out with my friends less frequently than I did previously.

You should attend at least one live event so that you can meet other people in your niche. It is fine to meet people over the internet but you really feel the connection to people when you meet them in person. There are many events that take place throughout the year. I now use most of my vacation days to attend online marketing events. From my personal experience, it has been definitely worth the sacrifice.

You should also get a coach or mentor. This is the one thing that I waited much too late to do. You need someone to guide you and keep you on the right path. If you think that you cannot afford one-on-one coaching, start with group coaching. This is generally less expensive and you can also determine if the coach/mentor is right for you. You can get suggestions for coaches from other people but you need to work with someone that you are comfortable with.

Can I Really Leave?

Once you decide to leave, you will more than likely have second thoughts. These may be delusions in your own head or comments from others. If you were brought up with the mindset to go to school and get good grades as a way to obtain a good job, then there will probably be many people in your life that won't understand why and what you are attempting to do. Don't let others kill your dreams or dictate what you do you in your life.

You will experience some fear that may be related to either finances or security. A lot of people in corporate America believe that there is some sense of security with their job. That was probably true previously, but I totally disagree with this. We are no longer in an era where you work for one company and then you retire with a pension. The days of pensions are for the most part over and people are laid off every day in corporate America.

Unfortunately, most people's lifestyle keeps up with their income so they feel trapped in their job. With an exit strategy and a financial plan, you can leave your job. Before you leave your job, try to reduce your expenditures and save money. Determine the amount of money you really need to survive. Don't forget to include money for benefits that you will now have to pay. If you can take advantage of COBRA, find out the cost of these benefits well in advance of you leaving your job.

You may experience a lack of confidence in your ability to actually be successful on your own. There are many skills that you developed in your corporate life that are directly transferrable to your entrepreneurial endeavors. Make sure that you have the proper mindset because that can be very detrimental to your success.

First Things First

I believe the first thing you must do in order to be a successful entrepreneur is to determine your why. If you think that making a lot of money will be enough to motivate you when things really get tough, then you are sadly mistaken. If you ask any successful entrepreneur, 9 times out of 10, their why is not just a monetary reason.

I have several reason whys. I want to be in control of my time. When I am completely free and working my online marketing business full time, I will be able to fully fulfill my dreams. My number one dream is to spend more time with my family and friends. I also want to have the resources to help them when necessary. I want to be a role model for my son, nieces and nephews so they know that you can make a decent living without working for someone in a traditional job.

I also have a dream of creating two non-profits. The first one would be in honor of my mother. She died from leukemia at the age of 49. Unfortunately, we could not find a bone marrow donor for her. She did undergo an experimental stem cell transplant in which the patient undergoes the same exact procedure as a bone marrow transplant. It was successful for a few months, but then the leukemia returned. I want to start a foundation that provides assistance to individuals who have to undergo a bone marrow transplant due to leukemia. This procedure is very expensive and requires months of recovery.

My father passed away in February 2013 at the age of 69. He had diabetes for many years which led to many other chronic diseases. I want to start a foundation that teaches children healthy habits so that they will not be susceptible to Type 2 diabetes as an adult.

My last desire also has to do with children. As someone with a technical background, it saddens me when I see how the United States is losing ground in Math and Science. There are so many children who think that Math is hard. I want to start a technology center geared specifically to girls that will teach math, science and technology. I want girls to think that these topics are fun, not hard and that they cannot succeed in them. I want to teach them about online marketing so that they can have their own businesses instead of looking for a menial summer job.

Things You Must Avoid To Be Successful

Once you decide that you are really going to pursue an online marketing career, there are a few things that you must avoid. The most important thing is to avoid BSOs. Now if you are new to this field, then you probably don't know what BSOs are. BSOs are "Bright Shiny Objects". Once you start to explore online marketing and sign up for various email lists, you will be inundated with offers. A lot of them are pretty inexpensive and the sales pitches are very convincing. All I can say is beware. I definitely went down this path and even today have to be careful. Only buy what you are actually going to use now.

You also want to master one thing at a time. There are so many facets to online marketing that you can easily find yourself going down one path after another. Concentrate on one or two things first. Master those and then move on to something new.

Lastly, you need to be careful with who you listen to. There are a lot of gurus and very successful online marketers out there, but they don't always agree on the approach to success. Find someone you resonate with and trust. Follow them. If you try to listen to too many people, you will become very confused and won't get anything accomplished.

Leave The Corporate World Behind

My online marketing company is called Leave The Corporate World Behind which is also the name of this book. My mission is to teach people in corporate America who want to get out of the rat race how to start an online internet marketing business that can potentially replace their income, allow them to control their own destiny and stop trading time for dollars. I am very passionate about my mission. I feel that I am uniquely qualified to help this audience because I am part of this community. I understand the pressures of their full time jobs and how to balance it with a part-time business.

Parting Advice

My passion changed over the years, but I took no action to adjust what I was doing to match my passion. My caution to you is don't wait to follow your dreams. Find a way to do what makes you happy even if it is only on a part-time basis in the beginning. Life is short and you never know when your time is up. I am excited about the new possibilities that are in front of me and you as well.

Adrienne Dupree is currently a full-time Program Manager for a government contractor, an author and a part-time online marketer. She has a technical background with a B.S. Mathematics, B.S. Electrical Engineering and M.S. Computer Science. Due to her technical background, she is very passionate about making sure that people are not intimidated by the technical side of their online marketing business. Her company, *Leave The Corporate World Behind, is for people in corporate America who want to get out the rat race, stop trading time for dollars and be in control of their own destiny so that they can start an online marketing business. She wants to show every person who is in corporate America who wants to get out of the corporate world how they can initially start part-time with an online marketing business. The goal would be to move them to a place where they can replace their full-time income. She is well equipped to really help this audience because she is part of this community. She understands the pressures of having a demanding corporate full time job and how to balance it with a part-time online marketing business. To find out more about Adrienne Dupree and Leave The Corporate World Behind and how you can leave the corporate world behind go to:*

http://leavethecorporateworldbehind.com.

On Again Off Again Entrepreneur
by Jeanette Cates

I was lucky enough to grow up in a "mixed" environment - my grandparents had their own bookkeeping and tax service, while my father was a good soldier in a hierarchical organization - the U.S. Army. I was able to see the contrasts and be equally comfortable in both environments.

As a young child I spent a lot of time in my grandparents' home office on the many times we stayed with them while Daddy was away. I learned early how to use a calculator, an adding machine, and a typewriter. I often stapled things for my grandparents - whether they needed them or not! There are even pictures of me sitting in my high chair stuffing pennies into coin wrappers as part of the family business.

I loved that Granddaddy and Grandmother got up and went to the "office" downtown, too. I thought it was perfect that they ate lunch out each day and seemed to know everyone in town. I liked going with Granddaddy to the local truck stop to pick up the shoebox of receipts, then separating them into stacks so that Grandmother could record them.

On the other hand, I loved being a military child. I liked the regulations and the set ways things were done. In high school, I volunteered as a Candy Striper and worked in the hospital mail room, sorting mail and updating regulations. It was all very regimented and very comfortable.

First Corporate Job

It was not a surprise to anyone when I decided to get an accounting degree. With my Bachelor of Science in hand, I was one of only two women hired by Arthur Anderson in their Houston office that year and began my career in auditing.

I hated it! Auditing was not what I had signed up for - I really wanted to be a bookkeeper. So when I married and moved to Germany with my Army husband, I left the auditing world - in spite of Arthur Anderson's offers to send me to language school and work in their German office. My friends thought I was nuts, but I knew I was not cut out to be an auditor.

Lesson Learned: Get experience in a field before you train for it. While I had experience in bookkeeping, I never spent a day even shadowing an auditor, so I had no clue what they did. I spent 4 years training for a job I hated!

Free Lance Teaching

As a military wife in Germany at that time, I was not allowed to work on the post. Working in town required a work visa so I didn't qualify there. But there was no restriction on teaching in the Army Education Center. The problem was - I had never taught anything nor trained as a teacher.

But that didn't stop me. I started teaching typing. I loved it! I added another class on GED Math. I loved it, too! I continued teaching part-time throughout our time in Germany, then in Korea. When we returned to Texas, I applied at the local college to teach part-time.

Lesson Learned: Just because you don't have training in a field doesn't mean you can't do it. Give it a try!

Full Time Curriculum Writer

One thing led to another and I was soon working full-time, writing curriculum. For six years I got up, went to work and wrote print-based lessons for 8 hours a day. It was interesting work, interviewing people who were professionals in their field, then turning that information into lessons that novices could use to learn to do the same job. I wrote courses on math, office skills, print shop trades, and a variety of other topics.

When we moved to Austin in 1980 my husband and I were both unemployed. We had been working on the same federal grant that was not refunded, so we both lost our jobs the same day. With three children, no jobs and no health insurance, we decided to move! Our parents thought we were nuts, but we knew that Austin was where we belonged.

I assumed I could get a job as a curriculum writer. After all, I had six years' experience and Austin is the education hub for the state. But it turned out that Austin is also a place former University of Texas students want to stay. So people with masters' and PhD's will do any job to stay in the city! I was "under qualified" for every job I applied for.

Lesson Learned: Experience may be a good teacher, but it doesn't always qualify you for the job. Back up your experience with education.

Part Time Bookkeeper

I found myself back in bookkeeping, this time working as an actual bookkeeper in a bookkeeping service. I was back doing the part of accounting that I loved - talking to the clients, recording the transactions. And at the same time, I started at the University of Texas to get my masters' degree so that I would have options.

One of the courses I took at UT was adult education. In that course we had to take a class on something we wanted to learn about, so that we would be in the learning role of novice. It was 1981 and computers were starting to appear on the scene, so I took a short course on computers in education. My world changed! I fell in love with technology and the impact it could have on education.

Lesson Learned: Feel free to explore new learning opportunities. You never know which will trigger a lifelong passion.

My Bookkeeping Business

Back at the bookkeeping office we were still doing all of the work by hand. I went to my boss and explained that we could do so much more, more efficiently if we just used one of the new computer systems. When she would have none of it, I quit that job, bought my first Apple II+ and started my own bookkeeping and tax service. In fact, it was the first personal computer-based bookkeeping service in Austin!

For two years, I built the bookkeeping service, working with clients just as my Grandfather had done: Picking up their records at their place of business, bringing them home to record them, then returning the printed reports to their offices. The business grew big enough that I hired an assistant to help with the books - and to watch the kids when they got home from school on the days I was at a client's office.

<u>Lesson Learned:</u> When you do what you love, it grows.

My Training Business

Between the bookkeeping business, taking graduate classes, taking care of a growing family and doing taxes I was crazy busy. But I couldn't turn down an opportunity to open a computer training company in another city!

For six months I and my husband commuted to San Antonio 4-5 times per week, hired 20 part-time instructors, then managed multiple training classes in that city, teaching out of a computer timeshare business. Naturally I had written all of the courses myself, while my husband had duplicated and collated all of the training materials. But six months into that venture, the company who had hired our new training company collapsed and we were out of business overnight!

Almost simultaneously an opportunity came up - actually two of them. The local community college wanted me to work part-time as their computer coordinator. It was only temporary they said, to fill in while their first computer coordinator recovered from surgery. I said yes. (Twelve years later I left that "temporary" job, which had become more than full-time by then!)

That same week I heard from the college, I was approached by a CPA who wanted to buy my bookkeeping and tax service. It was an ideal situation for both of us: He got a well-branded and established company. I got my first residual income in the form of monthly payments for the business, plus a percentage of the profits for the next three years!

<u>Lesson Learned:</u> Sometimes change happens quickly. Be ready to adapt.

Full Time College Administrator

I was now back to working just one job at the college and attending graduate school in the evenings. By then I had finished my masters but kept taking courses since there were so many exciting educational technology courses being created each semester. We were literally inventing the field of educational technology one semester at a time! And I had the advantage of working in it daily.

After six years of graduate school my husband finally pointed out that I had kept taking classes, even after I graduated. So I took Spring Break that year, wrote my dissertation and graduated with a PhD in Instructional Design - essentially now a professional in doing what I had done many years before - turning one person's expertise into a course to teach others how to do the same thing. I loved it then, and continue to love it today.

While at Austin Community College I had many opportunities to write articles and publish in academic publications. I also had multiple opportunities to speak at state and national conferences. The College gave me the freedom to do some consulting on the side, so it was very pleasant working conditions.

As the Computer Coordinator I managed the staff and locations for open-access computer labs on 7 campuses. I designed 4 of them from scratch and developed an expertise in ergonomic and efficient lab design. I also bought a lot of computers in the twelve years I was there, so I got to know all of the computer representatives well.

During my tenure as the computer coordinator, the college moved into the Internet world. Working with the University of Texas, I was in charge of bringing the Internet into the college, establishing procedures, and writing the policies for student and faculty use. It was great being on the cutting edge.

At the end of eleven years at the College, I took a three-month sabbatical. I did research, wrote, and generally reviewed my options. In spite of having a PhD, as a non-faculty member, I received no additional compensation or recognition for the degree, while my faculty peers enjoyed promotions and raises. Frankly, it wasn't fair and I knew it was time to start looking.

After my sabbatical I was required to work for the same length of time as I had taken off. I stayed to that day and not a day beyond.

<u>Lesson Learned:</u> Sometimes what starts as a temporary job turns into a full-time experience. Stay as long as you enjoy it - and not a moment longer.

Full Time Educational Consultant

It was scary to leave the comfort of the college environment, but I took a full-time job that offered both risk and excitement. SchoolVision of Texas was a new company with the Apple Computer education contract for all K-12 schools in Texas. They hired me to be their sales rep for the San Antonio region.

Now mind you, I had no sales experience. I wasn't excited about learning to do sales. But that was the job. I called on schools, showed them computers, helped them work out plans for labs and curriculum integration and sold them computers. I actually won my team's sales award one month! But my sales success was short-lived.

Within six months, they rearranged the sales force and took me out of it. Instead, they put me onto the newly-formed consulting team. Four of us covered the state of Texas, doing briefings, consulting, and demonstrations so that the sales reps could actually focus on sales. Now THIS I could do!

For four years my three colleagues and I travelled the state, border to border. We spoke at conferences, received top-level Apple training, and even went to Apple headquarters to complete Apple staff development training. It was a great job.

While all of this was happening, the Internet was being invented. Literally when I did my first Internet workshop, name servers were not used. You had to type in the IP address for the site you wanted to visit. By 1997, the Internet was in full force and Adobe PageMill, the first HTML editor, was the hot product.

Again, I went to my boss and explained how important the Internet would be to schools. I proposed a series of training courses we could offer to the schools. She didn't want anything to do with it.

Coincidentally contract renewals were coming up and the new contract included a non-compete clause that would prevent me from working in educational technology for three years after I left the company. Instead of signing the contract, I gave my notice.

Lesson Learned: Even when you love a job, sometimes the signs point in a different direction. Be willing to follow the signs into the unknown.

My Educational Technology Company

On May 15, 1997 I walked away from my full-time job and onto a plane for my first National Speakers Association workshop. That was my first full day of my new educational technology company.

This was not a last-minute decision. I had decided several months before that I was leaving on that day. My contract was set for renewal on June 1 and I didn't want to sign the non-compete clause they were adding. Since I knew I wanted to attend that specific NSA workshop, I knew that May 15 was IT.

But I didn't leave unprepared. I had already planned my next six months. I purchased five Macintosh laptops and five PC laptops, plus a server and an LCD Projector - while I still had a job to guarantee the purchase. The plan was to pack up my van, travel to a city, teach a workshop for teachers on How to Publish Your School Website for three days, then go to the next city.

I also didn't leave without laying the groundwork for sales. With my employer's permission (they were not going to teach anything that competed with my workshops), I made a list of every school district and teacher I had worked with in the prior four years.

So on May 15, I mailed hundreds of personal hand-written notes and invitations to attend one of my pre-scheduled workshops. I also invited them to contact me for consulting.

By the time I returned home after the weekend, I had business waiting for me. And that made all the difference!

Was it a lot of double-work to plan all of this and make all of the arrangements for multiple workshops, hotels, and events while I was still working full-time? Yes.

But I knew I didn't want to wake up my first day of "freedom" and realize I had to get out there and invent a business! That was downright scary.

<u>Lesson Learned:</u> Don't just leave your job. Plan for it. Prepare for it. Profit from it.

Educational Technology Consulting

Over the next three years I taught a lot of workshops, did a lot of consulting and spoke at a lot of conferences. I helped pioneer online K-12 education with several organizations.

Classroom Connect had a unique model. They held large multi-day conferences around the country for teachers. As an instructor for them I would teach two or three classes multiple times over the three days. Then we would do it again in another city.

Classroom Connect was also one of the first organizations to see that not all teachers could travel to one of their conferences. But they all wanted the information. So they started an Online University.

With a PhD in Instructional Design and my face-to-face teaching experience, as well as prior online learning experience, I was a logical choice to write and pilot some of their core courses.

I then leveraged that experience into creating the curriculum and core for the T.H.E Institute Online University.

One notable project I was hired to do was establish the Apple Learning Interchange, an online portal for K-12 educators around the world. With a team of 15 virtual contractors I hired, we created the site, loaded the initial content, and then built the online community that lasted until 2010. I had the opportunity to both present and train on ALI in several countries - all at Apple's expense!

<u>Lesson Learned:</u> Recognize your core skills and go back to them often. Not only does it feel good, but it's also easier to create from your core. Plus, the caliber of your products increases as you pull from your core.

The Internet Startup

I was happy running my own educational technology company, speaking around the country, so it took a lot to get me back into a corporate setting. But the temptation to be a part of the Internet Dot Com explosion in 1999-2000 was too great to pass up.

I joined Articulearn (originally CampusStream) as their Director of Professional Services. With both the CEO and their VP as former Apple reps I had worked with, I was very comfortable.

One stipulation of my contract was that I did not have to give up my business. I had built my online business quietly as I was creating my reputation in educational technology. I had learned to create websites, using HTML. I had established multiple websites and even taught classes to our local business groups on the importance of having a website. So I was unwilling to give that up when I went with the Startup.

True to form of the Dot Com era - we lasted a little over a year. During that time we had wonderful experiences. I traveled all over the country, consulting with clients and presenting at conferences. I hired and trained the professional services staff, included instructional designers and customer service reps. It was great experience.

<u>Lesson Learned</u>: Be willing to throw yourself into an experience to gain the most you can from it. Then be willing to move on.

Online Pioneer

As I left the Internet Startup, I knew that was my last job. Having been in and out of jobs for 30 years, I knew I was meant to work for myself.

I also knew that I wanted to be online forever. My passion lies in learning and teaching. The technology and marketing aspects of running an online business provide a limitless amount to learn. And for those of us who find it relatively simple to translate that information, teaching is the logical outcome.

I taught my first formal 12-week Coaching for Online Success in the Fall of 2001. I included interviews with good buddies Tom Antion, Robert Middleton, Fred Gleeck, and Alex Mandossian. I recorded the calls from the telephone onto cassette tapes, then sold the course as a stand-alone product.

As one of the first visible women in Internet Marketing, I was always in the minority at conferences and meetings. In an audience of 400 there might be 40 women, only 2 or 3 of which had already built an online business.

So it was a needed and natural progression to cohost the Womens Power Summit in 2005 with Alex Mandossian. Alex was the MC and only man allowed in the room. That conference and the one we did in 2006 changed a lot of women's lives. It focused on empowering them with the skills and attitudes they needed to become successful online.

During that same time I also spoke at multiple conferences and attended many more. If there was a conference on Internet Marketing, I was most likely there! Just as we had done when I was in graduate school and inventing educational technology, we were now inventing Internet Marketing!

Online audio was still relatively new and expensive. There were no social networks. So conferences were where you needed to be to learn the latest information. They were also where you formed the relationships that lead to later business deals.

Lesson Learned: Nothing takes the place of a face-to-face relationship. If you are serious about building your business, you must attend events.

Full Blown Business

With my attendance at so many events and the connections I made, it was easy for me to become visible online. I was one of the first people to use and teach about teleseminars. At the time, Alex Mandossian's Teleseminar Secrets was the hottest selling $2000 product online. My Teleseminar Basics, at $97, was the perfect alternative. We used to joke that his was the graduate program and mine was Kindergarten. Luckily a lot of people only needed Kindergarten to get started with teleseminars!

But that wasn't my first product! My first product was the recording of a speech I had given at a local meeting in the late 1990's on How To Use Email. I recorded it on my cassette, designed a cover insert, and then duplicated them on my boom box, one tape at a time.

Over the past 18 years, I have created hundreds of products and courses. The technology has evolved to be 100% digital and delivered online. And it's all gotten easier!

By 2010 I had built a highly successful, six-figure business online. I had a bookkeeper, webmaster, customer service rep and multiple contractors around the world. I was selling hundreds of products each month and had the highly successful Online Success Incubator, considered one of the premiere training programs for new online business owners.

I was speaking at several conferences per year and mentoring multiple people, many of whom went on to build their own six-figure businesses. I had achieved everything I ever wanted in a business.

Lesson Learned: Do what you love and figure out how to make money doing it.

The Crash

In May, 2011 everything changed. I developed a bad case of depression for reasons still unknown. I sat for days, doing nothing. I cancelled trips. I didn't talk to people. I didn't write emails. I didn't teach classes. I didn't create products. I stopped doing everything.

When you have an online business that has been set up correctly, it continues to function, in spite of your day-to-day activity. In fact, for the first three months after I stopped working, my business continued to grow! I was thrilled.

For the next three months, it remained steady with no decline in revenue. It wasn't growing, but it was declining either. I was more than thrilled!

It took six months before it started to decline, but being depressed, I didn't care. I let it slowly slide away.

Lesson Learned: Set up your business to operate on its own. Remove yourself as the center of everything. Establish procedures and hire people to carry them out.

Retire And Refocus

One of the characteristics of an entrepreneur is that they typically have a short attention span. They are passionate about what they are doing at the moment, but that focus fades.

One of the things that make online business so effective for entrepreneurs is that you can change focus, but still remain in business online. You can totally change your business model from consulting to passive revenue with advertising-based sites. You can move from being a successful affiliate marketer to being a product creator and vice versa. The possibilities are limitless!

Following my "crash" of 2011, I never regained the momentum I had. Frankly, my passion for the business was gone. I was tired of too many offers, too much change, too many things to learn new again.

So I looked around to see what else I could do online. And I rediscovered writing! In 2013 I wrote six books, several of which achieved best-seller status on Amazon. As I write this, I am on schedule to publish more than a dozen books in 2014, each with a product on the backend to generate passive revenue.

One of the projects I'm looking at is writing about models for retirement online. With the online area being so new, there are no models for people who have successfully retired online. In fact, many of the marketers I have talked to say they can't imagine retiring!

I have a different perspective than many of them, but then I'm 10-20 years older than most of them. I believe there will be many of us who choose to retire online, writing our own script as we do.

Lesson Learned: Write your exit plan. Will you sell your business? Turn it over to someone else to run? Sell parts of it and keep others? Change your focus? Your exit plan will serve you well whether you decide to retire or you have an unexpected emergency that requires you to leave the business for a while.

Leaving The Corporate World

Your journey from the corporate world may not be smooth. It may not be a one-time, one-way exit. As I've shown, you can come and go in and out of the corporate world multiple times.

The biggest obstacle to leaving the corporate world is fear. Fear of the loss of income. Fear of failure. Fear of making a bad decision.

Reduce your fear through preparation. Before you leave your job, make the big investments you need to make for your business, while you can still guarantee them with your current job. Set aside at least three, preferably six months' of income, so that you have enough to cover your expenses.

Remember that starting a business, even online, requires money. You need to buy domain names, pay for hosting, buy training courses, attend conferences, and hire help. These expenses are over and above your living expenses.

Yes, you can build an online business without those things, but it will take ten times longer. Plan to invest in your business and it will pay off for you.

Reduce your fear through education. Take several courses (one at a time!) to learn how to build an online business. Then apply what you've learned to start your business. Yes, you want to start your business while you are still employed.

Is it hard to work full time and build a business part-time? Sure it is! But if you are not willing to put in the extra time and effort now, there is a good chance you won't do it when you are running your online business. There will be times when you have to work many extra hours to get your business going or to meet a deadline. Learn now whether or not you are ready for it and you'll save yourself money and heartbreak later.

Reduce your fear by planning your exit. Know exactly what you will do before you leave your job to prepare for your last day. Go back and read what I did to get ready to leave my job and start my educational technology company. I did a lot of work prior to my last day of work!

Know what you will do every day for the first six weeks you are self-employed. Have a task list of daily tasks. Interview successful entrepreneurs and ask them what they do on a daily basis.

Reduce your fear by having cash-generating skills. While you may dream of a high-paying consulting business, most times it doesn't start that way. Instead, you have to build your reputation. You may need to get more experience before you can consult as you wish.

You may need to help someone create their videos before you can teach a course on video marketing. You may need to write articles for hire before you can build a publishing business. These types of experiences not only give you more credibility, but they also generate cash along the way.

As one example I taught the Internet Marketing Basics course for the Robert Allen organization in 2002. It didn't pay well, but it put me in front of a lot of qualified prospects. In fact last week, 12 years later, I did a consultation with a couple who took that course from me and have followed me ever since!

First Steps To Online Success

You've made your decision. You are leaving the corporate world. You've set the date. Now what? Here are the first steps I recommend you take.

1. Find ONE person you resonate with who offers coaching and sign up with them. The biggest waste of time many new people online make is to sign up with 3 or 4 "coaches" then spend all of their time trying to sort out the different approaches.

2. Do EXACTLY what your coach tells you to do. This goes against our grain for a couple of reasons.

First, you are leaving the corporate world because you want to be your own boss. You don't want to follow someone else's direction.

Second, our Western educational system teaches us to research a topic, sort out the various points of view, then come to our own conclusion.

But when it comes to making money, these two perspectives cost you time and money. Instead, just do what they tell you. For the second online business you build, you can do it your way. For now, follow the advice you're paying for.

3. Plan to attend a live event as soon as possible, ideally with your coach. Nothing takes the place of personal relationships. Start as early as possible.

4. Learn to work at home. Many people are unsuccessful because they never learned how to work at home. When you work at home, you need to be as focuses as you are in the workplace. Don't try to do the laundry, run errands, and watch the kids while you are working. It won't work.

If possible, practice working at home before you leave the corporate world. If that's not possible, practice working at home on Saturday or Sunday afternoons. Learn how to close the door and tell your family they will need to wait.

If you can't do this now, you won't be able to do it later. And it will cost you time, money, and frustration. Learn this skill now.

5. Learn to track your success. You can't know whether or not you are successful if you don't have measures of your success. What does success look like to you? How many visitors do you need to generate enough optins for your mailing list? How many visitors do you need to your sales page in order to sell a product? How many products do you need to sell to pay the bills?

Set your criteria for success now, then set up a success tracker. I track my success factors daily. That means that on any given day I can tell you exactly how much revenue I have received, how many books I sold, and what marketing activities I completed.

These five steps will start you well on your way to building a successful online business!

I love helping people get started online! You can always find me at JeanetteCates.com and on Facebook or LinkedIn. I'd be happy to answer your questions and help you make those all-important decisions to start right online.

Best of luck in leaving the corporate world and entering the exciting world of Online Success!

Back to Sales Again
by Barb Ling

My name is Barbara Ling and I am 49 years young. I was born, bred and raised to be an engineer for perhaps the first 2 years out of college, and then become a housewife (my mom told me that every woman should have a job so she can understand what her husband goes through after a hard day at the office).

I majored in Mathematics at college and was the founder and president of the official Math Club. Interestingly enough, I also designed t-shirts as a fundraiser for it! :) Upon graduation, I landed a job as a computer salesperson for Tandy Radio Shack which lasted 1 month and 1 day (I couldn't sell my way out of a wet paper bag back then, and management had to wait for one full month to pass before firing anyone).

Not truly learning my lesson, I then tried selling insurance for Prudential. That lasted perhaps 3 weeks? Door to door sales were definitely NOT my cup of coffee (although I did learn about the art of direct mailing from them).

Soon after biding a fond farewell, I was hired back at Radio Shack as an Educational Support Specialist. I maintained Radio Shack computers for NJ, NY and PA and happily drove all over creation, wreaking miracles with the TRS Model 80s (would you believe you could network them?).

Time passed (2 years?) and then my dream job finally arrived. I had applied to AT&T/Bell Labs 10 times since graduation. 10 rejection letters I received! Not giving up, I sent in the 11th application and struck gold; I was hired as a data analyst for AT&T up in White Plains. This was 1988.

AT&T and Bell Labs

AT&T and Bell Labs were definitely made for me. I fast discovered that my techie abilities could be put to superb use and taught myself systems administration, scripting skills, but alas, NOT corporate politics. This dearth of my skillset led to several negative corporate battles and instilled in me a desire never to undergo such things again.

Corporate America Exodus

In 1995, Bell Labs (by then it had transformed into Lucent) decided to undergo a downsizing. Not, not that – it was described as a "right-sizing!" Back then, companies were willing to pay employees to take a bonus package and leave. Bell Labs gifted me with several thousand dollars and I waved a fond farewell.

No Preparation

Utterly nothing. I was rather pregnant at the time and figured I'd now become a happy housewife and raise my family.

Alas, I didn't take into account post-partum depression. My child was born but the depression started right after birth. When she was 17 days old, I hired a nanny and began my company, Lingstar. That depression lasted until the birth of my second child and I haven't looked back since (I have 4 wonderful chlidren; my first will attend college this year (can't believe 18 years have passed!)).

Continuous Reinvention

Since 1996, I have continuously reinvented myself depending upon where my interests lay at those specific times. Over the past 18 years, I have taught:

- SEO
- Website Design
- eBay selling
- Product Creation
- Teaching children how to read
- Digital Photography
- eMail marketing
- Facebook
- LinkedIn
- Social Blogging
- Weight Loss
- Fitness

- Internet Realtor training
- Internet Recruiting training
- Motivation

I found the most success happened when I would focus on what interested **me** and not what others thought I should do. This is a never-ending lesson.

Overcoming the Obstacles

The biggest obstacles are:

- Self-discipline
- Finding the best path that works for you
- Remembering to take care of your health as well.

Having a set schedule every morning definitely helps the self-discipline. To find the right path, I recommend a huge amount of research, watching and learning. Three of my favorite free groups for this are:

Experienced Marketers at Internet Marketing Superfriends at:
https://www.facebook.com/groups/imsuperfriends/
Beginners/Under the Radar Marketers at The IM Inside Track at:
https://www.facebook.com/groups/theiminsidetrack/
Authority Marketing at Perking Up Profits at:
https://www.facebook.com/groups/perkingupprofits/
That last group is mine; my focus these days is centered upon authority marketing.

What To Do First

Find a mentor/pay a coach/join a quality paid community. Folks with experience can open doors way sooner than you can achieve on your own. Back in 1998 when I was the premiere trainer for Internet marketing, my mentor Bill Vick introduced me to all of his colleagues and it took off from there. That was my first 250K year.

Next, invest in an autoresponder and a business domain name. The autoresponder is how you'll build your list, and your business domain will be where you'll showcase your talents and what you have to offer your future customers. This is a critical business investment; don't go with free solutions here. You want to brand **you,** not your providers.

Finally, start to build your reputation online. Every day, take time to answer 5-10-20 questions in a targeted niche forum. Get known as someone who always can find out the answer. Those are the people from whom your customers want to buy.

Things To Avoid

Avoid the products/ideas that simply do not harmonize with your karma. If they're not you, don't force it.

Also never buy blindly. It's tempting to get on the HYPE bus but in the vast number of cases.... it will simply turn into a Bright Shiny Object that does you zero good. Conserve your money for the paid community or mentor.

Parting Inspiration

You and you alone own your success. If something isn't working out for you, nobody can fix that except you! Follow the Law of ProAction and kick fate in the right direction.

Your bottom line will thank you for it.

To find out more about Barbara Ling, check out: http://barbaraling.com.

Creating And Then Leaving the Safety Net by Karon Thackston

I have been in love with advertising since I was six years old. I used to watch the Frito Bandito in commercials on television on Saturday mornings. I would say to my mother when she would ask what I wanted to do when I grew up. "I want to do that!" as I pointed to the TV. I was referring to creating ads.

That's how my love for advertising and marketing began. To this day I'm fascinated by the way different words, ideas and approaches to advertising can have on the responses of customers.

That's what drew me to copywriting. I began to notice the different words and phrases, the way the text was formatted, the images that were included on web pages and a lot of different aspects played a big role in whether or not people would convert.

All through high school - when I had to do projects for marketing classes or other classes that even were remotely related to advertising - I would always take the lead on the projects and almost always made A's.

I majored in marketing when I was in college and knew from a very early age that this is what I wanted to do with the rest of my life.

CORPORATE AMERICA

The first job I held that involved marketing and advertising was working for the University of South Carolina's student newspaper in the sales department. I would call on clients, service the accounts when customers wanted to place ads in our student newspaper (called "The Gamecock"), create drafts of the ads for the graphic arts department.

When I left the University of South Carolina I went to work for the in-house ad agency of a local women's clothing manufacturer that operated a chain of wholesale outlets. As the Advertising Manager for this chain of stores I was responsible for creating all sorts of different advertising and marketing campaigns including radio, television, newspaper, magazines and the like.

This was long before the advent of the Internet so there were no websites and no online advertising to include in the mix.

From there I worked for a couple of advertising agencies and other in-house marketing departments for a variety of different companies. I just wasn't happy doing it the way that other people wanted. I wasn't content with having a schedule that was defined by other people or being forced to stay in the office when I finished the work that I needed to.

My husband and I were talking about starting a family. I really wanted to be able to stay home with the children that we might have one day so I began to investigate ways to create an online business. Because the Internet was becoming a mainstay in corporate America this idea seemed very possible.

If I could find a way to work from home and reach people all across the country I felt pretty certain that I would be able to make enough of a living to at least cover my (then) current salary.

Little did I know just how exciting or how successful I would later be by starting my own company and working from home.

PREPARATION TO WORK FROM HOME

As I began to prepare to work from my house, I kept my eye out for furniture that I could use in my soon-to-be office. I would pay attention to website design and to the ways that other people handled their online businesses.

I asked a lot of questions I joined forums and groups. There was no social media then, but there were other ways that you could get in touch with online business owners to ask questions and find out what was working for them.

I also checked on what was required legally for me to start a business from my home. This included what taxes I would be responsible for (if any), licenses required by my state or my county, and anything else that I would legally need to be aware of before starting a company.

MAKING THE TRANSITION

I started my company before I left corporate America. I would get up very early in the morning and answer email and work on client projects. Then I would take work with me to the office and - when I had time on my lunch break - I would continue to work on client projects. At night I would do the same thing again: back on my computer answering emails, writing copy and pulling projects together.

I was very blessed to be in a situation where someone in the company (who had similar responsibilities to mine) turned in her notice on the same day I was thinking about turning in mine. I waited a few days for them to plan on how they would distribute this other employee's responsibilities because I knew some of those would fall to me.

Then, about three days later, I turned in my notice. This gave me a little bit of leverage to hopefully work out a plan that I had concocted.

I explained to my supervisor that I would be happy to stay and work half days for two months while she interviewed and hired someone to handle my responsibilities and the responsibilities of my coworker. After that person was hired, I offered to train the new hire for an additional month.

This gave me a safety net. I could grow my business gradually over the time that I was working half days and still have a little bit of a steady paycheck coming in from the part-time work I did for my previous employer. This allowed me to make a very smooth and safe transition from my day job to my online company.

MARKETINGWORDS.COM

Marketing Words is a copywriting agency. We conceptualize and produce copy for practically anything related to online business. We create website copy of all different forms from e-commerce product descriptions and other short text all the way to complex landing pages that are used in email campaigns or PPC.

We also create emails, social media posts, blog posts, landing pages and many other types of online copywriting.

Marketing Words has worked with lots of companies of all sizes including Gorton's Seafood, American Boating Association, Entertainment Publications and more. We conduct copywriting training for those who want to learn to write their own copy and we provide onsite and online custom training seminars for corporations.

You can find us online at www.MarketingWords.com.

BIGGEST OBSTACLES

The biggest obstacles to leaving the corporate world seem to be fear and lack of money. There is an enormous amount of fear especially for people who have worked in a corporate environment and had a steady paycheck for many years.

The thought of owning your own business is very romantic. Lots of people love the thought of being able to wake up when they want, to work as many hours a day as they want and to schedule time off whenever they would like.

However when it comes down to putting your money where your mouth is, a lot of people are simply terrified of letting go of that steady paycheck.

And who could blame them? It's not a comfortable thing to do. I speak from experience. I was also terrified of letting go of that steady paycheck, but I was tired of all the trappings corporate America brought.

When I'd finally had enough, I overcame the fear. I was either going to leave the company I was working for without having another job (because I was so fed up) or I was going to leave in order to start my own business. The risk for either was pretty much the same at that point so I decided to make the leap.

There's also fear of failure. Not just the fear of starting, but the fear of having it taken away from you or losing it in some other manner. Nobody likes the idea of putting a lot of time and effort into something you're trying to build and not having it work out. Planning can play a big role in overcoming these fears. Instead of taking a blind leap, make as many preparations as you can so that you can ensure you have an action strategy when you start your business.

If you think you're working toward starting an online business (even if you're not sure) go ahead and begin to put some money aside. Start a little fund to pay for things like office furniture. Even if you buy used office furniture you have to have somewhere to conduct your business. Then there are other necessities including computers, scanners, printers, letterhead, website design, etc.

If there's a possibility that you can work part-time and make a smooth transition like I did, I strongly recommend that you do it.

FIRST THINGS FIRST

One of the first things I recommend to new online business owners is hiring a coach. This is something that was not available when I first started my online business and I wish it would have been. I could have made much faster progress and been much more successful in a shorter period of time. It is invaluable to have someone who has already walked the path to take your hand and show you the way.

The hesitation with hiring a coach is always that – in the beginning – most people are working on a limited budget. You already have so many other things you have to pay for. However, if you try to navigate the waters of online business all by yourself, and do everything yourself, you're setting yourself up to get burned out very quickly.

Everyone doesn't have the same talents and strengths. That's why the second thing I recommend is that you hire a virtual assistant to do the things that you aren't able to do or don't want to do. Again, people really hesitate when it comes to hiring an assistant because they see this as an expense. However as your virtual assistant (VA) is doing the technical things (or whatever it is that you are unable or unwilling to do) you are free to carry on with moneymaking activities in your business.

Look at it this way, how much moneymaking time would you lose trying to teach yourself WordPress website development? In a shorter period of time and for a lesser amount of money you could hire someone to do that for you while you continue with moneymaking activities in your business.

Contrary to popular belief you cannot successfully handle everything yourself. There simply are not enough hours in the day.

There are also some things you should avoid as an online business owner. I started out as basically a workaholic. I was up very early; I would work until very late Monday through Saturday and rarely took any time off. I don't suggest you follow in my footsteps. This is a rough road to ride and you can get frustrated very quickly by working this much.

I suggest you take time off, set office hours, play on the weekends, take vacations with your family or your friends, and have some fun. You need time away from your business so that you can come back to it refreshed, renewed and rejuvenated.

IN CLOSING

I absolutely love being an online business owner. I can't think of anything else I would rather do. This is perfectly suited for me. It is not perfectly suited for everybody, however. I strongly recommend that you take a trial run of having your own online business before you make a final decision that this is what you want to do.

You could easily take on some pro bono work with whatever type of business you wanted to start. As you're working through these complimentary projects you'll be able to see what's involved with running your own online business. Maybe it's for you, maybe it isn't. It could be that being at home all day - away from life people - is something you are not able to cope with. It is possible that the freedom of being able to create your own schedule turns out to be a trap. Some people simply aren't able to self-motivate and meet deadlines.

Don't assume, just because you hear online business owners talking about their perfect lives and how much they love what they do, that it well-suited for everyone.

On the other hand, I'll say again, I love my life as an online business owner and I wouldn't trade it for anything! If you think you have what it takes then I encourage you to go for it with everything you have. It took me 18 months of working approximately 14 to 16 hour days before my business was up and going to a point I was comfortable with. Don't fool yourself. You're in for a lot of work, especially in the beginning, but the rewards can absolutely be overwhelming and unbelievably awesome!

From Insurance To WordPress
by Paul Taubman

My name is Paul B. Taubman, II and I founded the website, http://INeedHelpWithWordPress.com. As the site name describes, I help people with their websites that are created using the popular platform, WordPress. If people want to know how to create a website completely on their own, I teach them what needs to be done, step-by-step. If someone wants it created for them, I will do all the work so they can concentrate on their strengths and build their business. This is my passion, and I love doing it!

I didn't always have this awesome website building and teaching job (and I have trouble calling it a job); I am currently working for an insurance company. Technically, my title is Senior Software Developer at the insurance company, and what I do basically comes down to getting various computer systems to talk to each other and share data. My area of specialty at the insurance company is known as Reinsurance. Reinsurance is when an insurance company gets insurance on insurance that they have sold. This is a very simple definition, and in reality it is more complicated than that. Out of the entire company, only a handful of us really understand how the reinsurance systems work.

I have been in the insurance industry ever since I graduated from college. I was recruited by an insurance company, although I never had any thought or dreams or aspirations to go into the insurance field. But, as things turn out, I was a lifer in that industry! After 26 years of doing this, it was time to find something different. I was always really good at what I did, and I enjoyed the people that I worked with. The camaraderie among my co-workers was great! The environment was friendly, we felt like we were doing meaningful work, and making a difference (well, within the organization, at least. I mean, it was not like we were curing cancer or anything).

Though a series of changes in management, the culture at my company started to change. Originally my bosses all had a background in insurance. This makes a huge difference when you are explaining what needs to be done. As time passed, a top manager was recruited and after time, he started to bring in his colleagues from his former employer. This happens all the time and came as no surprise. The part that was bothersome was the fact that these individuals came from an industry that was outside of insurance. Many of them felt they could apply what they knew from their former job directly in their new position at the insurance company. It would be analogous to a horse breeder deciding one day to breed snakes! Sure, some of the concepts were similar, but there are a lot of differences which were overlooked.

These new people really made work unbearable. I was frustrated at the inefficiencies that were becoming rampant. I found myself explaining myself over and over on the same topics because people did not want to understand. Overall, I knew I had to get out. While I have a pleasant disposition, I was discovering that I was getting angry and frustrated.

All during the time I was working at the insurance company, I was building websites for people. A lot of my clients were what I would consider, "community service." These were places that I was volunteering at and giving back to my community. Another client was a non-profit organization. I was building these sites as a means of helping out by giving back to the community. This was back in the html days of websites. I started to hear about "e-commerce" so I took a course that dealt with WordPress. I immediately saw the value of being able to change content easily without having to know any technical code! I was so hooked that I converted the sites of all my clients to WordPress.

During the course, I created a website called, http://AllAboutGratitude.com – gratitude was my passion. As I went through the course, fellow classmates would ask if I would build a site for them because they either got behind, felt the course was not for them, or because of some other issue. I quickly built a 'secret' sales page on the Gratitude site; this page advertised my WordPress services. Before I knew it, I was making money helping people with their sites! I knew I had to get it off of my gratitude site and so, http://INeedHelpWithWordPress.com was born.

At this point, it was just a hobby that was bringing in some extra cash. Nothing was steady, no real advertising was taking place. I was just happy to get some random work, here and there, as I continued to develop my WordPress skills.

I started to think about what it would be like to do this full time. I loved the idea of working on various tasks at once and having several clients at a time was very exciting for me. I wondered what it would take to let me leave my job... at this point, it was still a pipe-dream.

I was invited to speak at an event as a WordPress expert! Now I was entering the big leagues! I was getting more exposure. People were seeing me as the go-to person for their website. This brought in more work and more money. I began to think and plan on what would be needed to REALLY do this full time!

I started to work with a mentor and a coach. I started to learn how to market myself better. I was the unknown expert, but growing quickly. I started speaking more, getting more exposure, and reaching out to more people. By doing this, additional work would come in. I was slowly building a sustainable business.

New products were created and sold. Partnerships were formed and additional courses were created. I was ready to start a continuity program, or membership site, so WPSiteHelp was formed. At this site, people can join a monthly training session where they can have their specific questions answered to problems they are having. The answers are explained on a live call so they can see exactly what needs to be done. This really helped build a steady income. I knew the end of the insurance job was inevitable once this started gaining momentum!

Finally, I selected a date that I decided would be my last day working my 9-5 job! My work was cut out for me if I were to leave my 6-figure job and have it be replaced by working for myself. I needed a plan of attack for where the income was going to come from. What would be needed as far as sales were concerned? How many members would I need in my monthly membership program? How many websites would have to be created each month? How many courses sold? I was put into planning mode!

As of this writing, I have my date in mind and I am on track to leaving! At this point, I can taste my end date! It was suggested to me that I write my resignation letter today, and date it for the day that I know I will be leaving! When I am finished writing this chapter, I will be typing up my resignation letter and I will keep it in my desk drawer waiting to the day it is dated! That will be a great day for me!

While I look at what both lies ahead of me as well as what is behind me, I realize there are certain obstacles that actually prohibited me from leaving sooner that I have planned. There were things I could have done, actions that could have been completed earlier, and above all, thoughts that I should have banished from my mind; these all would have assisted me in submitting my resignation sooner than I am currently planning.

The biggest obstacle that comes to my mind, is... my mind! For the longest time, I was stuck with the belief that I needed the sense of security. I wanted to know that I have a steady income coming in every other week. If I slacked off one day at work, it did not necessarily matter in the grand scheme of things as I was ensured that I will still get a nice chunk of money direct deposited into my checking account on payday

Leaving my job means that I am 100% responsible for bringing in the income that I would need to survive financially. Through the years as my salary would increase, my lifestyle would grow along with it. My wife and I like nice things. We like having the liberty and ability to do just about whatever we want without have to be concerned about money. Truth be told, we probably eat out too much; we probably do not need to get some of the things we buy; I did not need to get a new motorcycle. But we can, and we do.

Knowing that this cushy paycheck might not come in is a HUGE obstacle from stepping out on my own. I will be 100% responsible for replacing that income if I do not want to change my lifestyle.

Another obstacle that I faced was the fact that I was trying to build my business while I was working full time! I often ran into the proverbial Catch-22. In order to leave my job, I needed to get more clients. However, the more clients I got, the more time it took from my personal time. And this personal time was getting shorter and shorted the more I was building my business. My time was limited, yet I needed to get more business. There were sometimes when I felt like I was getting squeezed from both ends.

My vacation time was spent attending conferences, speaking, and teaching around the country. While I always enjoyed myself at these events, it certainly was not a complete vacation. It takes effort to attend a conference and be there mentally. At the end of most conferences, while I may be excited at the possibilities that arose from the weekend, I was also physically and mentally drained. Most of the time, I did not have an extra day to recover; I had to be at work the next day.

Finally, the biggest obstacle that I needed to overcome was my family. When I started talking about leaving the security of my traditional 9-5 job (which started earlier than 9 and ended past 5), it was not taken lightly. While my family supported me in my efforts and what I wanted to do, there certainly is some anxiety around where the income would come from, would the income be on a regular basis, would the bills get paid, what about the mortgage, etc. Heck – it is only normal to be concerned about those things – I certainly was and it was my decision to leave my job!

After several discussions and over time, we came to an understanding and a relatively calm feeling that this could work. I always had full support from my family in what I was doing, so it was just a matter of time before the comfort level that was needed was achieved. In reality, taking the time to try to explain and convince my family that this was a viable solution also provided me with the extra reassurance that I could do this! It was a mindset change not only for them, but for me as well.

As I look back, I cannot pinpoint a time that I said to myself, "I am going to do this online thing full time." It was a gradual building – the feelings were inside of me and I knew that I wanted to do what I really enjoyed doing. Having the flexibility and freedom to work on what I want is a very freeing feeling and is very much different than being told what projects you have to work on. As work become more and more (what I called) insane, it became more apparent that I needed to get out.

I think that was the first step in my transition. I had a vague idea that I would be leaving at some point. I did not know when, I did not know how, but I definitely knew why! At that point, I was working on a goal to extricate myself from my job. I had it in my mind that I would eventually be leaving

– no definite date was set, but I started to think about life without my day job.

That started me in the direction of determining what I needed to do in order to become successful online. Initially, I had a coach to help guide me along the way. I knew that if I were to accomplish my goal, I needed someone to guide me along the way. I wanted someone that had been where I was (in a job) and left that job to be online full-time. This person knew the path to take and could lead me in that direction. I did not want to waver back and forth, try to accomplish my task through trial and error, rather, I wanted to have someone to guide me down the unknown road I was about to take.

Next I had to get the right mindset of what it would be like to leave my job. It was a fun and enjoyable feeling when I would go into work with my 'secret' that I would be leaving this job at some point in the future. It was knowing that I was a "short-timer" that helped me get through some of those miserable seeming days. Things that would bother me in the past, soon became non-issues; after all, I knew that it would not directly affect me in the long term. I knew that I would not have to deal with that annoying person much longer. I didn't know how long that would be, but I knew it was not going to last long.

Picking a date was the next important step in my success. Having an actual date and knowing when my last day would be was a key element to solidifying my goal. Until this point, I would have to call what I was doing a dream. Once I put a date on it, it became a goal; I had a definitive target date in which I had to prepare to resign. This was both an exciting time as well as a time of butterflies in my stomach.

At work, I have a whiteboard where I would put a number in the upper-right corner. Each day I would come in and the first thing I would do is erase that number and replace it with a number one less than what was there. This was the countdown until my last day. It served as a visual reminder of my target date and the date I would be on my own.

During this time, I developed a financial game plan to help get me to where I need to be. I did not want to simply pick a date and leave! I wanted to make sure I had a road map of what I needed to accomplish financially in order to maintain my current lifestyle. To me, this was a key element. Having a plan of what I needed to do, the number of websites to create, products to sell, members to enroll, and affiliate sales, provided me with a tool to follow in order to obtain my goal. The funny thing was that when I laid it all out, it seemed much easier than I thought. Now, "seemingly easy" is much different than "being easy" and I knew that I still had a lot of work to do to obtain those numbers. And it was a start!

Feeling comfortable with these simple things in place, I was able to move ahead with my plan. Once I had these things accomplished, I knew I was going to leave my job. I am looking forward to that day coming up in a handful of months!

Looking back from where I am now, I realize there are a few things I wish I did earlier. First and foremost is making the decision and setting a date earlier than I did. It is said that there is never a good time to leave your job if you want to, and I certainly found a lot of reasons not to leave it...It is not a good time because we just bought a new house. It is not a good time because my wife was not working. It is not a good time because my wife's job is funded by a grant and if the grant runs out, she could be out of a job. It is not a good time because we just put in a patio. It is not a good time because the winter is a slow season. There is always a reason why it is not a good time. While it would not be prudent to throw out all logic and reason especially in such a dramatic decision, it should be realized that you need to follow the advice of Nike and just, "Do It!"

Pick a date and move towards it. Use that as your goal. If your circumstances dictate that you change the date, do so with careful consideration. There is nothing wrong with that! Having a date will help clarify a lot of things for you. It is much more definite than just saying, "I am going to be leaving my job someday."

Another thing to avoid is trying to go about this on your own. No man is an island. Get the help you need to help guide you and avoid potential mistakes. Follow the advice of someone who has traveled the path you are taking and let them be your guide. It is not uncommon for the solopreneur to think that he/she can do it all alone. It is easy to get trapped behind the keyboard all alone and build a business.

Here is something else you should avoid: Don't leave your job until you know what you are doing. This may seem like common sense, but I know a few people who quit their day jobs to "make money on the internet." They were starting from scratch. They knew either nothing, or very little. The rationale they had was that if they quit their job, they would have all their free time to learn and become successful! While this may be true, having an online business is NOT a get rich quick business. It takes time to build a business online and that is AFTER you know what you are doing. Learn the fundamentals. Get good at bringing in the sales dollars. Prove you have a viable track record and can support yourself before giving notice to your boss.

Right now, I feel like I am living a double life. One is my 9 to 5 day job, and the other is my online business training people how to make money from their websites. My day job knows very little about my alter ego, but they are soon going to find out about it. I am looking forward to the day when I submit my letter of resignation. I can't wait to answer the inevitable question, "Where are you going to work? Where did you get a job? What company?" I look forward to seeing the look in their eye when I simply shake my head back and forth and say, "Nowhere – I have nothing lined up. I'll be working from home for myself."

Online Business: Here I Come!
by Robin O'Neal Smith

My Dream

Relaxing by the pool while sending clients messages. Sitting on the beach enjoying the sunshine while handling social media. Traveling around the world taking pictures to sell or use for graphics. These are some of the things I want to be able to do and call it work.

Does it sound like a dream? It is my dream and some day it will come true! I'm still employed full-time and love my job, but I'm building an online business so I can someday leave this job with a good income and have a lot more flexibility to travel and work anywhere in the world.

Ever since I have been a child, I have been a dreamer. Many people thought my dreams were far-fetched, but I have managed to make many of them come true. From the man I married to the house I live in, to the places we have vacationed. At some point they were all a dream, one that some would have said was impossible.

Impossible is not a reality for me. Just about anything is possible if you believe in it, are willing to work hard to make it happen and have patience.

I know my dream of leaving a full-time, structured job behind will be a reality in the near future.

Who Am I?

I'm a mom, a wife, daughter, sister, friend, hard worker, project manager, director of technology, teacher, volunteer and employee.

I'm married to the love of my life and my biggest supporter. We have an 18 year old son who will be graduating in a few weeks and heading off to college in the fall. I love being a mom and feel that parenting is my most important role in life. Every decision I make as a parent will affect the future.

When my son goes to college, I will fill a lot of the void with my business. For the past year, I have put traveling and other business endeavors on hold to enjoy his senior year with him. So the world needs to look out come September...I will be dedicating many hours to making my business grow.

My parents live about a quarter of a mile from me and it is great to be so close. My father has a chronic illness and is in and out of the hospital often. I wish I could spend more time with them. Another "Why" for working from home.

I volunteer with my son's school through the band boosters and with my church. I also volunteer my social media services to the Pennsylvania PTA. I feel everyone should give back to the community. I have been blessed with so much, it is only right to return some of the good to others.

I adore technology, but it can be mind-boggling and confusing at times. The fun is finding ways to use new technology to improve what you are already doing or to save time or to create something you were unable to create before. I don't need to have the latest and greatest, but I like to stay in the know and ahead of the curve.

I enjoy photography and pictures, digitally enhancing photos, created pic-quotes, graphics, and writing. In my free time I like to scrapbook (but I'm years behind), travel (not enough vacation days to travel as much as I would like), cook (love trying new recipes and making great food, but time again limits these opportunities) and kayak (river kayaking is a great deal of fun, I'd like to purchase my own kayak but not sure I would have enough time to use it.)

The most daring thing I have done is zipline in Colorado, 150 feet above ground, over a river with a bear in it! Ziplining makes me feel totally free; I can't wait to have more time to spend doing this activity. I also enjoy white water rafting but don't get the opportunity to do it enough.

As a worker, I enjoy opportunities to be creative. I'm persistent, pay a lot of attention to details, and like the planning of things.

From Medical Professional to Entrepreneur

I once read, "You will have multiple jobs in your work lifetime, changing approximately every 7 – 10 years." This has been true for me. I have evolved.

I worked in the medical field as a respiratory care practitioner, but was tired of sick people. It was a secure job, (there are always sick people) but I was bored. I liked the emergency and critical care parts of the position, but they were only a small part of the job. Most hours were spent going from room to room giving breathing treatments. While a bit boring, it was tolerable, but the part that got me was people would be all upset if I was a minute late for their treatment, but before I would get out of their room after their treatment they were heading for the bathroom to smoke another cigarette. (Back when hospitals still allowed smoking on the premises.) I just felt what I was doing wasn't making a big difference and I needed more of a challenge.

So I toyed with the idea of going back to school to get a teaching degree. My heart wanted an elementary degree but my head told me to get something more marketable. (Good decision for me!) For every elementary position there are hundreds of applicants. I decided to go for business education since that would open more doors. If there were no teaching jobs, I would have skills businesses wanted and would be able to find a job one way or another.

Many people put obstacles in my way or tried to talk me out of going back to school. I remember going back to my high school to get my transcripts and the guidance counselor telling me that going back as an adult was hard and that he knew of no one who was successful at it. (Like that would stop me, just added fuel to my fire!)

Some of the people I worked with at the time thought I was crazy. Why would I want to do that when I already had a good job? Even family members were questioning my sanity.

The one person who was behind me 100% regardless of what I decided was my husband. He never wavered. Just said over and over, "If it is what you want, I will support your decision. I will adjust, we can do this."

So, I went back to school to become a teacher. I had only been married a few years and didn't feel it was fair for my husband to have to support me and pay my way through college, so I continued to work full time. I worked night shift and then went to school during the day. When I think back, I must have been crazy, but it all worked out. I completed my degree in three years and continued on for my master's degree.

During the time I was working and going to school, I averaged about 4 hours of sleep a day. Not optimum for success, but I made it work and was on the dean's list several times. This whole experience taught me what you can accomplish when you are focused and passionate. When people would say it was impossible, it just made me want to prove them wrong. No matter the roadblocks, I just told myself to "Stay focused. Keep your eyes on the goal."

It helped me to realize you CAN do anything you set your mind to. Yes I had to say no to a lot of things in my social life. Yes it was tough for my husband and me to have so little free time together; yes I missed some important events. But I proved to myself that anything is possible.

After graduation, I did some substitute work and then landed a part-time teaching position at a great school. I continued to work part-time at the hospital through all of this. The following year I was made a full-time teacher and left my part-time job at the hospital.

I taught business education, basically computers for several years, then took a position as a teacher technology trainer, and then moved into the Director of Technology position for the same school district. I have been there for 22 years with a year off for maternity leave. I will be making another job move this summer to the CIO (Chief Information Officer) position in the same district.

Transferable Skills

So what do I actually do in my current job? I am in charge of planning, decision making and purchasing technology for the district. I also plan and coordinate teacher technology training. Handle a million dollar budget and coordinate the work of 6 employees. I'm responsible for a lot of state reporting and making sure everything is submitted online in a timely manner. Our district web page and the five school building pages as well as our online presence on social media are my duties as well.

When I move to my new position I will take the parts of my current job that I love the most, social media, web page design, and administration of some software programs with me. I will also get to do more writing and data analysis along with public relations work. So even though I will still be in a full-time job I will be doing much of what I want to do when I am working for myself. It will be a great way to end my time as an employee. Skills I have learned through my training for my business are transferring into my full-time employment and things I have learned as an employee will transfer into my business.

Eventually I want to leave my full time job to run my own business. But I make a great salary with wonderful benefits and until my business can support that same lifestyle, I will work two jobs.

What is my WHY?

Why do I want to leave if I have a great job that I like? Well, I want to have more flexibility in my scheduling. I want to be able to stay up all night working on a project that I'm passionate about and then sleep part of the following day if necessary. I want to be able to work 3, 12-hour days so I can take time to be with family when they need me. I want to be able to work from my deck, my office, a hotel room, or by the pool. I want to be able to go with my husband on trips, yet still be able to work when I need to.

Taking family members to the doctors in the middle of the day, having a spontaneous lunch with friends, spending more time with the children in my church, are all important to me.

I also want the pleasure of creation. Creating products and things I know are of value and will help others.

I'm a hard worker and actually enjoy working, but I want to be able to do the kind of work I enjoy with clients I adore when and where I want to do it.

Currently I'm confined to someone else's schedule and someone else priorities. I need to dress according to a specific dress code and put at least 8 hours in a day. (I'm often there 10 or more hours.) You could say I want the freedom of being my own boss!

Preparing to Leave

To prepare myself for eventually leaving my current job, I have done and will continue to do a number of things to make it a smooth and successful transition.

First thing was determine how much money I would need to be making to leave my current job and maintain my lifestyle. Although I could get by on much less, would I be happy? When I make the move I do not want to have regrets and wish I had better prepared. So I made the decision to continue with both jobs till I was making a certain amount.

The second thing was to take several inventories and personal profiles to make sure I had the personality to eventually be disciplined enough to work from home. This is a biggie since a lot of businesses fail because the owner just wants to play and have fun and can't discipline themselves to do the work.

Then I started learning a lot of things. Took courses and learned the skills I needed to build an online business. This is where I made quite a few mistakes. Yes I needed to learn the ropes of my new endeavor and the skills were necessary, but I went overboard. I was in perpetual learning mode for far too long. In my effort to learn as much as possible I paid for far too many courses in too many different areas and wasted a lot of time with repetition and taking courses in things my business was not ready for yet. At some point you need to just bite the bullet and start doing. You won't know it all, you will make mistakes and learn as you go, but you need to get out of 100% learning mode and get into action mode.

Making connections was the next step. You have to know people in the business and have connections that are willing to help you. This might mean attending local meetings or going to conferences. For me it included travel to various conferences and workshops.

Another thing I did to prepare was start saving some money. You need to have a little bit of a cushion to fall back on if you plan to leave your full time job with benefits. Doesn't have to be a huge amount, but enough to carry you over a month or two if the need arises.

I started to think how I would provide for myself the things my employer has been giving me. Benefits such as life insurance, health insurance, and others. Depending how much you make, this could equal your salary and you need to take it into consideration.

After you take the steps to plan and prepare then you need to start doing. You have to create the business of your dreams and make the dreams a reality.

For me this involved two different avenues. My first business is Be Social, Get Success. It is a social media business that focuses on content, copywriting, graphics and podcasting. I always loved Facebook and other forms of social media and decided that might be a great place to start a business. I love working with photos. My favorite jobs are creating custom covers for Facebook and pic-quotes for Facebook and Pinterest. You can find my business at:
http://www.besocialgetsuccess.com

My second business, I fell into quite by accident. I was struggling to lose some weight and a friend approached me about Plexus Slim. It is a powder you mix with water and drink once per day. It improves the chemical balance of your body and helps your metabolism to function properly and either lose or gain weight depending on your needs. I used the product and found it to not only help me lose weight but help with a lot of other things like energy level, fatigue, fibromyalgia, arthritis, etc. After using it for a month, I decided to share about the product and people started asking where they could purchase. So I started an online business selling the product. We carry the Plexus Slim product as well as other health and wellness products. My personal page focuses on a general healthy lifestyle, family, recipes, and business.

Obstacles Can Be Stepping Stones

As I move closer to my dream of running a full-time online business I know there will be some obstacles to leaving a full-time job with good pay and benefits. I'm hoping the planning and preparation I have put in upfront will make it a smooth transition. Society has trained us to feel we have made it when we have the security of a full-time job and take home a paycheck with benefits.

I know working a business part time while still a full-time employee will be difficult at times. Trying to squeeze it all in will be taxing, but so much better in the end. It will give me time to build up my business so I'm sure it can support me and it won't just be sink or swim.

Another biggie will be what other people think. I will have to be very thick-skinned, when people start making comments that I'm crazy for leaving a full time job with benefits. It will be important to be confident that I am doing the right thing even when everyone else has doubts.

Adjusting to not having a boss tell you what needs to be done would be difficult for some, but I deal with that in my full-time job so I'm not concerned about that.

Time management is difficult for many, but if I can manage it while working full-time I should be able to do it part time. I think disciplining myself to do the tasks I like the least but need done in a business will be the toughest.

Getting Started

Through my experience, I have found you need to do three things when you are getting your business off the ground to be a successful online entrepreneur.

The first is to know your WHY. Why do you want to be in business? Why are you willing to sacrifice to make this a success? Who or what is your WHY?

The second is to know how you want to help people. What service or product will you be selling?

And the third is to know who your target market is. Who will you help? Who will be purchasing your goods or services? The better defined your target market, the more success you will have.

Entrepreneurial Pitfalls

If you are starting an online business, there are some things you need to be aware of and avoid. They can suck you in, eat up your time, and doom you to failure if you don't get a handle on the situation.

1. **Shiny Object Syndrome** – Everyone is selling a product online. It is easy to think you need to buy that product and learn about that new topic to be a success. So you buy, buy, buy and never implement. You have 30 courses or products on your computer that you haven't touched. Each shiny new thing catches your eye and you never fully complete and implement any of them. Avoid this like the plague. Make sure you are making money in your business from anything you purchase before buying something else.

2. **Following Too Many People** – Following too many experts or coaches will give you conflicting information. Follow too many and soon your inbox will be overflowing and you will have no time to work on your business, because all you do is manage your email. You won't have time to read everything, but what you do read will be conflicting. Then you wonder who do you actually believe? Which advice should you use? It is much easier to limit those you seriously follow from the start.

3. **Trying To Do It All Yourself** - As your business starts to grow, people often feel they need to do everything themselves. After all, you are not making a lot of money and you don't want to spend the little profits you are making on another person to help. This type of thinking can keep your business very small. Most people I have talked to have confirmed that once you outsource to others the things you dislike doing, are not good at doing or just don't have time to do, your business grows much faster. We can't be an expert at

everything. Allowing someone else to handle those things we are not good at or dislike gives us more time to work in our business on the things that we are best at.

4. **Lack of Organization** – You have to be organized or your business will run you! Create processes and procedures for the various things you do and handle in your business. This will eliminate headaches and stress. The more organized you are the less time you will waste. This is especially true at tax time!

5. **Self-Limiting Beliefs** – We often create our own glass ceilings. We feel our business will be a success if we are just bringing in $200 or $2000 a month. We never allow ourselves to think "BIG." We minimize our talents and abilities and often try to stay in our comfort zone. This type of thinking will keep your business small.

Advice for the Newbie

The best advice I can give someone who is starting their business online is to think long and hard about the life you want. Make sure your business is a fit for the life you want.

All work and no play make "Jane" a boring person! Schedule down time if you must, but make sure you have time away from the work. Devoting time and energy to the relationships in your life is important.

Know your WHY and remember it when the going gets tough. Use your why as your personal motivator and take action. Don't sit on the sidelines waiting for someone to put you into the game! Walk on the field and play. Only you can do it. Only you can make the decision of when to leave your corporate job behind. If you plan and prepare, when you do leave you will be ready to jump into a new successful adventure.

The Path To Success Has Many Lessons To Be Learned
by Debbie O'Grady

I grew up in a small town in Western Massachusetts - a blue collar town. General Electric was the main employer and it's where my Dad worked from the time he was 19 years old. When I graduated from high school, I was able to get a job working in the G.E. factory too. I remained a factory worker for about 8 years, first in Massachusetts and then in North Carolina. During this time I did all kinds of jobs, including driving fork lifts, running lathes and saws, and working on an assembly line. I finally decided, when I was 26 years old, that I wanted to do something more than just go to work in a factory every day, so I applied for student loans to go to college to get a bachelor's degree. I quit my decently-paying job and four-and-a-half years later, I had my degree in hand and was offered a job that paid double what I had made working in the factory. I'd say that was a darn good investment of my time and money. This first job out of college was my introduction to white collar work in corporate America. I spent the next 25 years working my way up the corporate ladder from software developer all the way to management level. The position I enjoyed most was project manager. I had a team of people and together we would work on a project to create what the customer requested. I loved being in a position where I could mentor junior team members and stretch them to take on more and more challenging positions that led to higher pay and promotions.

My experience as a manager in corporate America taught me the importance of mentoring and coaching the members of my team. I learned how to help people find and cultivate their strengths; to grow and broaden their outlooks; to stretch for their goals and be the best they could be. I felt I did things a bit differently from the other managers because I didn't wait for yearly reviews to "see" how each person was doing in achieving their career goals. Instead I asked for accountability on a more frequent schedule so each person could review and see the progress they were making towards accomplishing the goals they had set for themselves. Without that frequent accountability, those longer term goals tended to be forgotten and sometimes even lost with all the day-to-day distractions and emergent challenges needing to be handled. It was great to see that a high percentage of my team were promoted and took on challenging new positions.

After about 25 years in corporate America, I was getting frustrated and irritated working for managers that didn't seem to care about growing their team the way I did about growing mine. I had learned early in my corporate career to not be "the complainer." If I didn't like something, I usually figured out how to fix it or if that just wasn't possible, to move on. It was beginning to feel as though this was the time to move on.

I had always dreamed about having my own business but had no idea what I would do or how I would accomplish it.

One day, I mentioned my dream to a colleague and he suggested I think about being a consultant. I had been thinking that if I were to start my own business, it would be something completely different from what I had been doing in corporate America. I hadn't really thought about doing the same thing as I had been doing but as a consultant. I could take on the work and the clients I wanted. Once that thought was in my head, I couldn't shake it. I started getting excited about the possibilities that might be out there for me as my own boss and I began researching information about starting my own consulting business.

I had a well-paying job, so I knew I didn't want to just quit and then figure it all out later. I took my time and did my research so when the time finally came for me to walk away from corporate America, I did it with a lot of knowledge about what was expected of me as a consultant and business owner. That's the first bit of advice I would give to anyone asking me about going to work for herself or himself. Do your research about the kind of work you want to do. Understand what is required and expected of you in that position and as a business owner.

When I first left my corporate job, I went into business with two partners and we had a contract lined up that quickly grew to where we needed to hire employees to help us. At the end of two years, we had grown our company from 3 to 12 employees and were bringing in $1.2 million dollars in revenue per year. That was a very good start for a small company, but one day I realized that I was back to working for others. Even though I was one of the owners, having two partners meant I was still answering to someone else (two someones in this case) and I really couldn't do what I wanted to do. So once again, I felt I needed to move on to something else. But I had been bitten by the entrepreneurial bug and didn't want to go back to corporate America, so I decided I would go it alone as a consultant.

I made one big mistake this time that I had not made the last time. I did not do the research before I quit my well-paying job. I had recently moved away from the area of the country where my network and all my contacts were located. Once I was on my own, I realized very quickly that I did not know how to go about finding work or letting people know I was available. That was a big eye-opener for me and it's my next bit of advice for you. Learn and understand what you need to do to find clients. It's not true that they will come looking for you – you have to understand where they are and make sure they know about you and what you offer that can help them.

So I had to learn Marketing and Sales. I don't think I really knew it was called Marketing. I only knew about advertising and sales. I even knew I should have a website but had no idea what I could do with it. I found a great book called "Book Yourself Solid" written by Michael Port, and from that book I learned the foundational steps I needed to take to find clients. That book also introduced me to the world of business coaching. I got to meet Michael Port and attend the first class where he taught a small group of us how to coach and how to teach his Book Yourself Solid program. We became certified Book Yourself Solid Coaches.

So now I knew how to attract clients for my consulting business and I could coach and teach others how to do this for their business. I was so excited about having this knowledge and being able to share it. I made the decision to postpone moving forward with my consulting business and instead decided to train Michael Port's Book Yourself Solid methods. I continued to attend training courses and expand my coaching skills.

My business continued to evolve and today I teach women who have had a successful career working for others how to build a successful business of their own. My business offerings are focused around accountability – leveraging accountability to achieve your goals – as well as business coaching and training.

My absolutely favorite offering is our Glorious Global Gatherings, where a very small number of business owners gather at beautiful locations around the world for a 3-day Mastermind Intensive full of learning and sharing of business expertise and experiences.

The biggest obstacle I encountered to leaving the corporate world was thinking that I was more secure working for a large company than working for myself. I believe more and more people are realizing this is just not true. I had to get past that, and I don't know why it took me so long to see. After all, every time the contract I was working came to an end, I had to find another contract and interview for the position I wanted for myself. And since I was a manager and felt responsible for my team, I took on the added responsibility to help my team members find new positions. That was how it worked. It was each person's individual responsibility to research the openings within the company and find their own position from one contract to the next. Once I accepted that I was no less responsible for looking out for myself in my supposedly secure corporate job as I would be owning and running my own business, it made leaving to start my own business a whole lot easier.

The one thing I did not have to do in corporate America that is a requirement for my own business is to market the company. In today's world, you must have an online presence no matter what your business is. Therefore, you must learn some online marketing techniques from the very beginning to make your business a success. The world of online marketing is vast and varied and can be confusing, frustrating, and even a bit overwhelming for the newcomer. The advice I give to any new business owner or anyone thinking of starting their own business is to hire a Business Coach. Honestly, if I had not found Michael Port at the very start of going into business for myself, I would have been lost for a very long time. Having someone introduce and guide me into the online marketing world was truly the best thing that I could have done for myself and my business. I was so very lucky that it happened right at the very beginning. I still made a lot of mistakes but I had the right mindset and still, today, I continue to hire some of the best coaches that keep stretching me and ushering me to higher and higher levels.

Don't try to do this all on you own – you just can't. I'm not saying you need a partner. I'm saying you should have a coach to begin with and then a team to help you with some of the things you just are not good at doing. Your team can be part time. These are the experts like an accountant, an administrative assistant, a technical person, a graphics person, maybe a writer, a social media manager, and a marketing or business manager. Each of these skills is needed to help run and get your business seen by your target audience. If you have no idea how to do something, you need to either learn how or hire someone else to do it. Learning how to do it yourself can be great and possibly a lot of fun but be aware, it takes time away from you doing the actual work of your business.

That's my parting advice: understand what it is that your business needs to be visible to your target market and hire the experts to do that work. Because I came from the corporate world, and for years had a team of experts to handle the different positions on the project, I understood this way of thinking. It took me a while to remember that I cannot, and do not need to do it all on my own. I'd be a lot further along my path to success had I remembered and hired my team from the beginning of my business career.

I wish you the very best on your path to success!

Debbie O'Grady teaches women who have had successful careers working for others how to build successful businesses of their own. She teaches what she has accomplished herself. After having a successful career in Corporate America, Debbie moved on to build not just one but several successful businesses. The first was a consulting business Debbie started with two partners and built into a $1.9M business in only two years. She sold her share of that business to her partners and proceeded to build her own six figure consulting business. Today, Debbie still runs the consulting business and has also built the online, virtual business that powers her passion to help others do the same.

Known for her patient yet firm approach that holds your feet to the fire, Debbie's clients call her "The Queen of Accountability." As a former Project Manager, Debbie uses her planning and monitoring skills to teach you how to set Goals and Action Steps that stretch and keep you moving forward. In a loving and encouraging way, she mentors and guides you with practical insights and experienced suggestions to be productive and build your own successful business.

Debbie conducts virtual Accountability and Coaching Programs for clients worldwide as she too travels the globe. Debbie also offers private 1-day intensive strategy sessions and group multi-day Glorious Global Gatherings in some of the world's most beautiful settings, like Ojochal in the southern Pacific region of Costa Rica. You can learn more about Debbie and her program offerings by visiting her site:

http://RevenueRecharge.com

From Banking to Online Business Consultant by Nicole Dean

Who Is Nicole Dean?

There is so much I could say about myself. But, you probably don't need to know that I love roasted Brussels sprouts or that I can say the alphabet backwards, so I'll try to find a few interesting and helpful things related to business that will help you to get to know me in this short space.

I was born and raised in Wisconsin in a very small town of about three thousand people. I went to college in Wisconsin, as well, and married my college sweetheart. He and I decided to go on an adventure so we headed to Portland, Oregon and lived there for 8 years. That is the point where I worked in corporate America before starting my own business.

In 2003, we were up for another adventure, so we packed up the house, the kids, and the cat and moved to Pensacola, Florida.

My husband went through two difficult layoffs, one was two weeks after our daughter was born in 2001, so I decided to start finding ways to create my own business to be able to contribute to our family and not have all of the worry and pressure on his very capable shoulders.

It took time, but in 2005, I started to see some consistent income coming in as I created websites in varying niches.

From there, I took what worked and I learned how to recreate it over and over again. I invested in my business, and put my heart and soul into it, until my husband was able to choose not to work for a few years, as my business brought in more than enough for our family. He's currently home with me, and I love being able to spend time with him.

My Mission is To Make the Web and the World a Better Place – and, Hopefully Have a Lot of Fun While Doing It. I enjoy work very much, but live to spend time with my much-adored husband, my two silly children – and also my two crazy puppies, Einstein & Luke.

I love to travel and have a great belly laugh that can be heard in a very crowded room. I'm also a bit geeky (have been to a Star Trek convention). But I've got a super soft heart and I work with orphans (including helping adopting families with the process) and I also foster dogs that are in transition from an abused or neglectful situation into new loving homes. I also love doing jigsaw puzzles with my Gramma every chance I get.

Banking Operations

While I lived in Portland, fresh out of college, I worked in Purchasing and Operations for a 50 branch bank for several years. I transitioned from the Purchasing Department to Operations where I assisted with writing the bank manuals and I helped to manage all of the many forms and documents used by the branches and all of the departments, too. I was able to travel and I really loved my job. It served me well as I learned how to write effectively and quickly so that both a Bank Executive felt that the policy was written well, but yet it was clear enough for a 19 year old bank teller to pick up the training and walk through a potentially complicated situation.

Leaving Corporate America

At that point, life was really good. We had our first born and my boss was great about letting me transition to part time. But day care costs were high, and then my husband got a huge raise at the high-tech company where he worked, so I decided to take a few years off to focus on my son. Little did I know that 9/11/2001 was right around the corner and our world was about to change. Nine days after the towers went down my daughter was born. Two weeks after that as the high tech industry went into a panic, my husband's department was closed. We went from one really good income to no income overnight.

Preparation for Leaving Corporate America

I was in a position where we were starting a family and I wanted to be home. My transition came later, actually. When my husband lost his job, I was happily at home. I went into transition mode more at that time when I realized that I needed to be bringing in some money and I couldn't just enjoy being a mom. Starting my own business was the fastest and best way for me to do that.

My Online Business

I am an Author, Popular Speaker, Successful Blogger and Podcaster, and a Business Consultant to really smart people. I help Online Business Owners, specifically Coaches, Bloggers, Trainers, and Authors to be more profitable. Throughout my business, I provide resources, tools, shortcuts, and done-for-you services for each of those people to help them to be more profitable in less time.

I teach my students to set financial goals, but to also write down their lifestyle goals, as well. This ensures that they are building a business that aligns with the way they want their lives to look in 5 or 10 years, rather than creating a job where they are working for a crazy person – themselves.

You can find out more about me at either:

http://NicoleontheNet.com

Overcoming Lack of Confidence

The biggest obstacle that I see in people, and I faced it myself, is confidence. I lacked confidence in myself and I lacked confidence in the business model. I mean, really, the internet was just a fad, right?

Seriously, though, there was so much junk online that I also had to face well-meaning family and friends telling me to avoid the scams and that nothing I did was legitimate and I would never build a real business. I had to follow my gut and my heart and put blinders on to the people who were working their jobs who wanted to project their own fears onto me. So, I eventually even had to tell my husband to just trust me, trust my instinct, and to just let me see what this "internet thing" would develop into. Like many, I promised him that, if I didn't succeed in a specific amount of time that I'd give up. I think he finally realized that I might have built something pretty amazing when I started making more money than he did.

When I started, thankfully I made it my goal to find people who were where I wanted to be and to find a way to connect with them. I joined paid mastermind groups where other serious business people were brainstorming, and I hunkered down and absorbed as much as I could. I asked a lot of stupid questions, and wasn't afraid to let pride keep me from moving ahead.

As for specifically transitioning from the corporate world, don't spend a year trying to avoid making the wrong decisions. Just move ahead. Take action, see what happens, get feedback from smart people, and adjust. My business today does not look anything like it did when I started over a decade ago. It's evolved. Yours will, too.

Also, don't put off marketing. I see lots of my very smart friends spin their wheels because their site "isn't ready yet". Let me tell you, your business will NEVER be perfect and it will always be a work in progress. If you wait to promote it until it's perfect, you'll never make your first dollar online. Start doing and see what happens.

First Things First – Get A Coach

The first thing is to figure out who you want to learn from. Don't get stuck following 100 different people, because there are a million different ways to build a business and you'll get stuck with competing advice.

Choose one person who you want to coach you. Find out if they've got a group coaching program, or one-on-one coaching program and sign up. That way you'll have someone to ask when you get stuck, discouraged, or lost. And, at times you will need that.

Then, ask your coach for recommendations for outsourcing the things that you don't need to do yourself.

How do you know what to outsource? Here are some guidelines.

If you run into a roadblock that is something standing between you and profit, outsource it.

If you are against something that you need to only do once, like install a script or set up an account the right way, outsource it.

If it's something that's making you sad, frustrated and discouraged, outsource it so that you can focus on moving forward.

Once you get up and running, even if you can only work one hour per day, focus first on the things that make you money. Don't even open your email or Facebook until you've done one activity that moves you ahead. Then you can play.

Impulse Buys Avoidance

Avoid impulse buys. There are more shiny objects available to business owners than there are pennies in your bank account. No ONE course is going to make or break your business. If it promises everything, then run. This is another reason to have a good business coach. My clients come to me and ask "Do I need this?" I'll tell them whether or not it's a good fit for them, and oftentimes the answer is "No".

Parting Advice

The biggest pain as we get older is the pain of regret. Never think it's too late. Many entrepreneurs are having their "second lives" after retiring from their corporate jobs.

So whether you're a young mom like I was or you're a great-grampa who has a business idea or a book to write – there is room for you and there are people out there waiting to see your greatness shine. I'm one of them. So go do it.

You Can Do It!
Great Ways to Leverage
Your Corporate Experience
to Prepare For
Entrepreneurial Success
by Leslie Cardinal

I'm so excited to share ideas to help you move toward your business dreams! I'll start by telling you some of my own story because I want you to know that even if you have been in the corporate world for many years, as I was for twenty five years, you can still pursue your dreams to be an entrepreneur. Or, if you are new to the corporate world and need to stay in a job for a while (for example, to pay off student loans), you can still use your time in the corporate world to your advantage. I'll also share some of my favorite business success strategies that you can begin to use now, to start moving toward your business dreams and goals.

It may seem ironic, but I didn't set out to be an entrepreneur when I started my career. When I was in college studying engineering, my fellow students and I were mostly aiming to get a good job in the corporate world. Usually, these were well-paying jobs, even with only a bachelor's degree. The university even brought in companies so we could go for job interviews on the campus. My definition of success at that time was to get good grades, complete my degree, and then get a job working as an employee of a large company.

It's interesting to look back and realize that as a child I had some entrepreneurial interests. I was always looking for ways to make money. I did everything from babysitting, to shoveling snow, to collecting recyclables that had cash value, to trying to sell greeting cards. When I entered high school that changed. My parents strongly encouraged me to focus on advanced academics and college prep activities rather than pursuing any type of job or other money-making ventures.

Both of my parents worked, but neither of them worked in the corporate world. One was in the military and the other was an educator working for the local school district. Both were well educated with advanced degrees. The main career message I got from them was to get good grades, go to college, and then get a job that would pay well so that I could support myself. Neither of my parents encouraged me to follow in their footsteps, but instead to get a degree that would lead to a well-paying corporate job in a field like accounting or engineering.

I grew up during a time when there was a lot of attention on math and science, and young women were starting to be encouraged to study engineering. I knew that I would need scholarships and part-time jobs in order to pay for college. I was fortunate to win scholarships to study engineering and so I pursued that path.

I didn't have a particular passion for math or science or technology as a career, but I really didn't have another career path in mind. I knew that with my math and science abilities that I could probably succeed in earning an engineering degree. And, I knew that engineering was a respected professional path that would enable me to earn a good income. It was a practical, logical decision.

I enjoyed the challenge of college and learning. I did well in my courses, especially in my major which was Industrial Engineering and Operations Research. I didn't know anything about the day-to-day reality of working in an engineering job in the corporate world. I just followed the degree plan through to graduation. In reality I was completely focused on just completing my degree as fast as I could so I could graduate before the scholarship money ran out!

It never occurred to me to explore what it would be like to work in a corporate job, or to find out if I would like the type of work that my degree was preparing me for. I'm not sure I would have known how to do this if I had thought of it at the time.

In college, the scholarships I had earned paid the tuition but I still needed money for books and for living expenses. I had several part-time jobs while I was in college. I worked as a student engineer for a big oil and gas company. I also worked for the campus newspaper typing up the classified ads late at night to meet their publication deadlines. And, I did computer work for the university library.

But my entrepreneurial side started to kick in a little bit too. I did freelance math tutoring for other college students. This was great work because I enjoyed teaching and mentoring other students and helping them build their confidence and skills with math. And, the going rates for tutoring were much higher than the low hourly rate paid by the other part-time jobs. I liked the flexible work hours of tutoring, and being able to work close to where I lived.

As I entered my senior year in college, I started the accepted process of signing up for job interviews with the employers who came to the college campus. I never considered self- employment as an option at that time. It just never occurred to me, and none of my fellow students were pursuing this option either.

I received several job offers. I accepted an offer to work for the telephone company as a telephone engineer designing and managing the installation of telephone systems for businesses. For the first few months I immersed myself in learning the job, and that challenge kept me busy. There were some positive aspects of that first job. I had a supervisor who was an excellent mentor, and who gave me a lot of opportunities to grow. That first job was also part of a Management Development Program. This meant that I was able to attend a great variety of training classes in communications, problem solving, public speaking, and other "soft skills." I really enjoyed these classes and this started my formal education in non-technical topics that would later serve me so well in my entrepreneurial ventures.

After one year in that first job, I was assigned to another job within the company. Unfortunately, it was much less enjoyable, with a manager who didn't really want to have an employee to manage. This was a very difficult situation and very unpleasant. I knew I was going to need to find something better.

Looking back now, I can see that even though it was a painful experience, that job experience propelled me into an important part of my professional development. I became determined to find a career that would be enjoyable and fulfilling, and that would be a good match for my skills and interests. I didn't know how to do this at the time, but I was fortunate to find a good resource to help get me started. That first resource was a book entitled, "What Color is Your Parachute: A Manual for Job-Hunters and Career Changers," by Richard Bolles. I started working with the exercises in the book and that gave me a much needed feeling of hope as well as some beginning steps I could take.

Over the next few years I took several different jobs, working for The Federal Reserve Bank of Dallas, Texas Instruments, Texas Utilities, and Advanced Micro Devices. Although these were primarily technical jobs, I gained valuable experience and business insights from each job and each organization. Throughout this time, I continued to take classes and to read books to help me build my skills and knowledge and experience to help me as my career evolved. I was moving toward the field of Leadership and Management Development, and toward jobs that would involve corporate training and internal consulting. I ultimately ended up doing exactly this type of work when I worked for USAA, a large financial services company.

While at USAA, I was able to earn my masters degree under a tuition reimbursement program because the classes were relevant to the job I was in. I also paid for many other classes and training programs that would be useful in the career and business direction I wanted to pursue. I was able to start doing some freelance work on a small scale, coaching and consulting with executives and professionals and business owners in other industries, while I worked full-time at USAA.

Eventually, the company decided to do a major reorganization and this was a great blessing and opportunity for me because I was able to leave and work in my own business full time. Even though I would have preferred to be able to pursue my business full time sooner than I did, there were many benefits to do it in a more step-by-step process. I was able to use the time I was in the corporate world to prepare myself before I launched into full time entrepreneurship. It has now been more than twelve years since I left the corporate world and I look forward to many more successful years as an entrepreneur!

I'd like to share some of my favorite strategies for making the transition from the corporate world to your own business. These are the types of strategies I used myself and that I coach and mentor my clients to use. Be sure to use your own good judgment and decide which ones may best fit your own situation.

Start a journal or a file for your entrepreneurial journey

An easy first step you can take is to set up a way to keep notes and information to help you on your journey from corporate employee to entrepreneur. This is a simple yet powerful way to acknowledge to yourself that you are serious about your dreams of having your own business. If you enjoy writing notes by hand, use a tablet and your favorite pen and a file folder to begin. If you prefer, open a document on your computer and create a computer file to store your notes.

Take inventory of your skills and experience and interests

This step is another action that is not difficult. And, it will pay big dividends for you in several ways as you start and grow your business.

Start a list of the skills that you have. Make this a big list and include skills that you have used in your personal life as well as your professional life. One of my favorite resources for this is included in the excellent book "What Color is Your Parachute? 2014: A Practical Manual for Job Hunters and Career-Changers," by Richard Bolles.

Make a separate list of your life and work experiences such as the types of work you have done, places you have travelled, challenges you have encountered and handled, accomplishments, and topics you have studied. Many of these experiences can be useful for building your business, or for strengthening your confidence about all the things you have done and accomplished in your life.

In addition, make a list of your interests and hobbies. This can include everything from personal to professional interests, things you enjoy doing with your family, types of music you enjoy, and books you like to read.

Build on your corporate experience

Think in terms of leverage. How could your experience in the corporate world be an asset to you as you move in an entrepreneurial direction? I have found that working for several companies has given me insights into different industries, different leadership and management styles, different ways of interacting with customers and colleagues, and different ways of working with technology and information. The ideas and methods you learn in one industry can inspire you to adapt and create methods that will work well in a completely different industry.

What is your dream of life and work after the corporate world?

Take time to dream about the entrepreneurial life you would like to create for yourself. Do you want to have a micro business and work from your home? Do you want to start a small business that you can grow into a large business over time? Do you just want something that can be part time that gives you flexibility to care for your children or your older parent? Do you want a "brick and mortar" business with an actual physical office or store?

Clarify your "why"

As you are dreaming, look deeper to clarify the reason why you want to pursue an entrepreneurial life. What does it mean to you or represent to you? Sure, there may be financial goals, but look for reasons that are connected to your core values. For example, do you value time flexibility to allow you to be with your family, freedom to choose the projects or clients to pursue, opportunities for learning and growing professionally, or autonomy to do things in your best way? Each of these can be a great reason for pursuing self-employment.

Take classes, attend seminars, and go to conferences

Look for opportunities to build your skills while you are still in your corporate job. You may be able to take classes online or after work. Whether it is individual classes or a certificate program or even a formal degree program, there are many ways to learn the skills you will need in your business. Seek opportunities to learn, or to attend conferences, while you are still in your corporate job. If there is a way that these could be helpful to you in performing your current job well, explore the possibility that your company could pay for you to attend these learning opportunities. Even if it is not the regular company policy to pay for these expenses, it may be worthwhile to build a good case and propose it because of the benefit you will be able to bring to your company.

Look for business workshops and seminars offered by Chambers of Commerce or your local Small Business Development Center. If it is not against your company's policies, it may even be worth taking vacation hours to attend. Look for conferences related to your entrepreneurial goals and attend them if possible.

Also, keep learning about the technology you will need in your business. This includes basic computer and software skills, email and online search tools, social media, and smart phone skills. Take advantage of any opportunities your company offers to learn technology skills.

Start part-time, on the side

You may be able to work part-time in your new endeavor while you are still in your corporate job, especially if your new business is not a conflict of interest with your current job. Be sure to check your employee manual or company policies about this. There may be guidelines or limitations that you will need to follow in order to avoid jeopardizing your job. Some companies completely prohibit employees from having their own businesses. Others allow it as long as there is no conflict of interest and no company time or resources are used for your venture. Plan and design your business with your company's guidelines in mind.

Be creative and look for opportunities. You may be able to start your business on a small, part time basis. Or you may be able to work part time for someone else to learn about the type of business you may want to start in the future. You may be able to do some type of relevant volunteer work for a nonprofit organization to gain experience. Another option is to seek or create a part time internship (paid or unpaid) or even a temporary job rotation that will help you gain experience related to your business goals.

Build your savings and keep your expenses down

Your business dreams will require some money to get started. Reduce your monthly living expenses if possible, and build your savings to help prepare for the transition to your business. You will need to buy the basic tools, equipment, and resources for your business. But you rarely need to have the latest or most expensive or fanciest equipment when you are getting started. Look for ways to buy used equipment, to work from home in a corner of a bedroom, and to borrow books from your local library. Keep your expenses down, especially in the beginning of your business.

Take a good look at the benefits of having an online business

One of the best types of businesses to start is a business that you can do online, rather than a traditional franchise or "bricks and mortar" business. Online businesses are often much less expensive to start because you don't have the expense of a building and the other expenses that go with it. Starting a franchise can cost from $50,000 to $500.000 or more. Don't cash in your retirement savings to start your business. An online business may give you more flexibility about when and where you work, and you may be able to work from your home. There are many types of businesses that can be done online, so take a look to see if this would be a good choice for you.

It's okay to go back to the corporate world, if you want to or need to

Fairly early in my corporate career I realized that I would need to make a career change to find work that I enjoyed and that was a better fit for my style and personality. In the process, I took some time away from the corporate world to pursue some additional training as part of the career change process. To support myself financially during this time I worked several part-time jobs and even started a small business to generate income. This was my first real entrepreneurial venture, even though I didn't have any dreams or plans to pursue your own business on a full-time basis. I found that I enjoyed the flexible scheduling options of having my own service business. And I enjoyed learning about marketing and managing a business.

When I moved to San Antonio, I did a variety of freelance jobs until I was able to find full time job back in the corporate world. The corporate job served me well during this time, as a way to expand my experience, earn a good income, and have the benefits that were available. You may find that you need the structure or the benefits or the income of a full-time corporate job. It is okay to go back into that world. It may be for a short time, or you may find that it will be a better long term choice for you. Either way, the experience you gained working for yourself, learning about business, marketing your services or products, is valuable. None of it is wasted. You may find, as I did, that you are even more appreciative of good managers and more aware of the business side of things, if you need to go back into the corporate world after having had your own business for a while.

Plan for a business venture after retirement or downsizing

You may decide that you are unable or unwilling to have a small business while you are also working full-time in the corporate world. It is true that it does take time and energy to do both at the same time. If you travel a great deal or have a lot of family responsibilities, it may be very difficult to have a small business right now. Nevertheless, I would encourage you to look ahead and develop an option for a small business that you could pursue later, if needed. After you retire from the corporate world and take a bit of time to relax and "decompress," you may find, as many of my clients have, that you would like to do something interesting and stimulating with your time like starting a business. Or you may want the extra income that a business can provide, to enable you to take some special trips, or help with kids or grandkids educations, or just to boost your own retirement income.

Build your network and contacts

While you are still in the corporate world you can be building your network of professional contacts. Build connections with people in your current industry as well as in the industry your business will be in. Be sure you are on LinkedIn and steadily build your connections with past and present colleagues. Attend local networking events too, especially those that will fit into your current work schedule. When you are doing things with your friends and family, be open to meeting other entrepreneurial people and ask for their business card so that you can stay in touch with them. Look for ways you can be helpful to them, perhaps by sending referrals, or sharing a helpful article, or even just a note of appreciation.

Connect with your professional association

Find out if there is a professional association related to your entrepreneurial dreams. Visit their website and explore the options available for membership. See if there is a local group that meets in your area. Look for informal business and professional groups in your area too, such as networking and Meetup groups. If possible, go to some of their meetings as a visitor. You will meet interesting people and gather useful information. If a group feels like a great fit, you may want to join as a regular member.

Be selective about talking about your entrepreneurial goals while you are still in your corporate job

Surround yourself with supportive people such a mastermind group, action buddies, a coach or mentor. While you are still in the corporate world, you may need to look outside of the corporate world to find other people who share your entrepreneurial interests. You may also find it helpful to work with a business coach or a mentor to accelerate and smooth the process of growing your business and transitioning from the corporate world to your own business.

Watch for opportunities such as layoffs, reorganizations, early retirement options, job sharing, and part time work options

You may be able to have your own business on the side for a number of years, even if there are reasons that you need to keep working in your full-time corporate job for a while. However, at some point you may want to make the leap to go from corporate employee to full-time entrepreneur. If you can do it with some financial resources, that is ideal. Keep your ears open for the possibility of a corporate reorganization or layoffs or early retirement opportunities that might enable you to make the transition with extra financial resources.

Believe you can do it, strengthen your faith and belief in your dream

More than anything, keep building your belief that you can achieve your entrepreneurial dreams. Every step of the way, you will learn and grow and meet interesting people. Enjoy the process and realize that it may take some time to reach your goals. Whatever your faith, tap into it to help yourself stay energized and confident. Your dream is worth pursuing. You have gifts and talents to contribute to the world. You can do it!

__Leslie Cardinal__ is a highly regarded coach and mentor for leaders and business owners. She worked for many years in the corporate world before making the successful transition to her own business. She really enjoys working with people who are ready to leverage their corporate work experience to help them reach new levels of success and fulfillment in their own businesses. By expanding her work online she has been able to help even more people achieve the success they desire in their businesses. For more information and resources, you can visit: http://www.GrowYourBusinessNow.com

From IBM Technical Sales to Private Label Rights by Justin Popovic

About Justin Popovic

A quick back story about me is basically I am a Canadian business owner. I've been doing this for around five years. Obviously, prior to that I was in the corporate world working for IBM for seven years. That was my prescription of what I was going to do with my life. I went to college and obtained a computer science degree with the intent of going to the corporate world.

A few years in, I realized it wasn't for me so I started searching and eventually entrepreneurship became my chosen new path. I am the father of two boys, age 6 and 4. My wife's name is Jessica.

Other than business I enjoy fitness. I do cross fit. I've played a lot of sports. I like to travel with my family. We take a lot of summer vacations and do stuff together. Pretty much I live a limited lifestyle in terms of entrepreneurship, spending time with my kids and working out. That's basically all I do but it's fun and I love doing all those things.

IBM Technical Sales

I was a Technical Sales Engineer for IBM. That title means many different things, but effectively my job was to help sell licenses of high powered software. My job would range anywhere from prospecting to finding potential customers to setting up meetings for people that wanted to learn more about the software. I would then go to these different clients and arrange demonstrations and speak with their teams, project managers and executives. I would also do live demos and sometimes proof of concepts, as well as closing the sale and even doing post sales training.

I did a lot of technical training, traveling to all kinds of different locations and doing different training for our customers on site or in IBM training facilities. My role was basically anything from sales to training to very low level technical stuff as well. So, it was an involved job with a lot of different responsibilities and stuff to do.

I also had a big role on the sales side of things. We had to do forecasting and figure out what our numbers would be each and every quarter and what the plan of action was to close those sales. I was compensated to a degree on the number of sales we made, so selling and tech went hand in hand. This is different than most organizations where one person does selling and another person does the tech. I was the "go-between" that did both. It was a unique position.

My Decision To Leave Corporate Canada

There were a number of factors why I wanted to leave the corporate world. I would say the biggest reason that I left the corporate world was because I didn't want to be there. I didn't like doing it at all. It didn't suit me. I felt like I had to be there and it probably went back to earlier choices in life where I never realized I had options. I assumed from a very young age that you go to school, get a job and do those things whether you like it or not. As I got older and started exploring, I realized the power was in my control to change all of that and most of the things about the corporate world I didn't enjoy. I think the worst part was the overall feeling that somebody else was in control of how I spent my time, my days and what my activities were.

I was doing something I didn't want to do. When I became aware that I didn't have to do that anymore, that it was totally up to me, that's why I decided to change. It was the awareness that the power was in my own hands to do anything I wanted, so there was no stopping me from starting my own business or doing anything else for that matter. I had to adjust my lifestyle and my expectations, but I could certainly do all these things. Being aware that I was able to change was huge.

I also left because I had a bigger vision. I didn't feel like working in the corporate world. I could fulfill the type of legacy that I had in my mind to build something really cool and obviously to make a lot of money. I could make a lot of money in the corporate world, but could make more money as a business owner. I could choose to do more projects that were within my comfort zone, so to speak, although getting out of your comfort zone is important.

As an entrepreneur, I was in full control with total freedom to do what I wanted when I wanted, projects I wanted to take on and to walk away from projects that I didn't believe in, which wasn't necessarily the case in the corporate world.

Sometimes if you had a bad customer or bad situation, and even if you didn't like it you would be asked to compromise your beliefs or your standards, because you had to accommodate what the company wanted to do, whereas, when you run your own business you never have to do that you're in full control. Those are some of the major reasons why I did it.

The biggest one of all was that I would dictate who I spent my time with and where I spent my time and that comes down to family. Since quitting my job I've been home almost all the time. I only travel when I want to, whereas before I was always traveling to do the training. Now I've spent the last five years at home. My kids are six and four, so for the most part I've been around every day of their lives. I take them to school every day. I pick them up from school. We do all kinds of activities together.

I coach their sports teams and I'm involved. I don't miss a day with my kids that you can't get back. These are the most important years to spend with them. You can't necessarily do that when you work in the corporate world. You have to do a lot of traveling, at least in the role I was in. I couldn't be home as often as I wanted to be.

Preparation For Leaving The Corporate World

I didn't do much to prepare for leaving the corporate world, to be honest. The biggest thing I did to prepare was to develop the mindset of somebody who was risk-taking, bold, self-confident enough to actually walk away from the security of it all. I didn't necessarily have a great business plan or even a lot of entrepreneurial skills. What I did have was a huge desire, major hunger and motivation to go out on my own to do this, to give it my all and actually go for it, and not try it for a month and if that doesn't work I'll go back and get a job.

I was committed to doing it, so the biggest thing I did was to get my mindset to a place where this was the only option. I knew it was going to be hard and there would be a lot of difficulties. I would probably mess a lot of things up and maybe even embarrass myself, but I got myself to a point where I was okay with whatever was going to happen. However difficult it would be, I was prepared to meet that head on.

The only way I knew to do it was to read a lot of books, watch a lot of speakers, watch YouTube videos and meet people who had done this before. I flooded my mind with positive messages and stories of people who had done it or messages and stories of people saying these kinds of things are possible. This was to recreate a belief system that you really can do it, whereas before my belief system was very much dependent on the corporation and the security of needing a job, because I couldn't do this on my own. Now I have changed my mindset to say I can do it on my own. That was the biggest thing I did to prepare.

My Online Business

The biggest thing we do is provide content licenses to other companies and business owners. That means we basically create white label digital products. If you think of white label think of a tub of ice cream you buy at the grocery store. Very often the company that puts their label on that tub of ice cream is not the company that actually produced the ice cream. A third party produced it and they bought it and slapped their label on it. That's how many things work in the business world.

We do that online. We create eBooks, video courses, audio programs and all kinds of different training materials that don't have an author name on it. It means that our customers are other business owners who also train or provide information products to their clients, so our customers come to us to basically buy products off the shelf that they can turn around and repackage as their own, as though they created it.

We provide them with the ability to actually customize the products they get from us so that it does have their voice and branding. We're taking a huge chunk of the work and the cost out of producing those products. It's content licensing at a high level.

Obstacles To Leaving The Corporate World

I think for me there were a lot of obstacles to leaving the corporate world, but it basically boiled down to two things for me.

The first big obstacle was the money discussion. Usually people in the corporate world are making pretty decent income and they've built a lifestyle around that. So you need to be able to understand the implications of walking away from something like that, or at least planning to leave that. The second obstacle was mindset.

Let's address the money issue. The biggest obstacle is that when you leave your corporate job you no longer have this big income. There's a good chance that as you become an entrepreneur you're new at it, so you won't be able to generate the same kind of income that quickly. It's going to take you time to learn the skills, build your network, and learn how to sell under your own name before you can reproduce the same level of income.

That's okay. The question then is what can you do without? How can you reduce your expenses and change your lifestyle so that you can still quit your job to build your business. A lot of people can reduce the amount of money they need on a monthly basis, by cutting out things like TV, restaurants and any kind of unnecessary expenses that can be eliminated almost immediately.

It won't be fun but it's worth it because you're doing something that is important to you. You also need to figure out on a base level what you can do without and then after you do that, figure out how much you need to produce.

Obviously, if you're quitting your job and you don't want to lose those things than you need to make sure you have the money coming in to do that. Here's what happened for me. Once I quit my job very haphazardly and didn't necessarily have enough money coming in to cover all my expenses, I had a bunch of money saved up as a safety net for me. Once I quit my job I used that money to fund my lifestyle, even though I had reduced some expenses, while I built my business.

The bad news was that I ran out of money and there's a chance that could happen to you as well. I started getting into debt. I was using credit lines and credit cards to pay for my expenses while I still tried to keep my business going. In the meantime, what I needed to do was adjust many of my plans as an entrepreneur. Some of the things I was working on weren't bringing in the money that I expected so I had to take additional jobs.

For example, I did work for a local college doing courses for them and creating programs. I was earning money and it wasn't what I wanted to do, but it ended up working out great. I made great contacts and learned how to generate additional money for my business, outside my main projects. As an entrepreneur you need to be flexible and adaptable to the situation.

My best advice is that you need to be prepared to reduce the amount of money that you spend on a monthly basis and to get your business to a level where the amount of money you bring in will at least pay for what you need. Also, realize that many people do go into debt and have to cut into their own savings to build their business, which to me is a test of your commitment.

How committed are you to becoming a successful entrepreneur? Are you willing to spend a little of your savings or go into debt because you believe in this thing? If you believe in it that strongly than even if you go into debt, I believe you have the characteristics that it takes to succeed.

You are going to be tested repeatedly and there will be many times that you feel like quitting. You may feel like an idiot and that you shouldn't be doing this thing. You may think that you shouldn't become an entrepreneur because you had a better setup in the corporate world, even though you didn't like it. There will be all these reasons to go back to it.

That's where the mindset comes in. How much pain are you willing to endure to make sure you stick to your plan so you become a successful entrepreneur? To me that's really what weeds some people out. The people that stick with it, that persevere and have the most persistence, ultimately will build a successful business. It doesn't mean it's going to be easy.

What are you prepared to do? You'll have to go outside your comfort zone. I was doing things like giving talks in front of large audiences, probably before I was prepared, doing cold calling to find new gigs and new opportunities to make money, literally knocking on people's doors to ask if I could sell them things. Things I never dreamed in a million years I'd have to do I was doing because I had no other choice if I wanted to bring in the money for my business.

Again, all those things made me a stronger person, a more effective entrepreneur and pushed me to do things I never thought I would have to do before. So, if you're prepared to do whatever it takes and you're prepared to continually motivate yourself to go through all those pains and challenges, then I believe those are the biggest obstacles you'll overcome and you'll do well if you can do that.

First Steps

If you're just getting started, it doesn't matter if you're an online entrepreneur or an offline entrepreneur, you need to understand your skillset, talents and interests, but most importantly you need to understand your skillset because that's what is monetizable. That's how you can make money.

Sometimes in order to get a business going you'll have to do things you don't love because you have those skills. So, rather than to just give you generalized ideas I'm going to give you my exact story.

I was in the corporate world doing tech sales, computer software and my goal was to become an entrepreneur as a motivational speaker and a coach. I had zero experience in the coaching and speaking world, but I had lots of experience in the tech world. My skills included selling, software demonstrations, setting up software systems on client sites and training. I started my business trying to make money as the motivational guy, but I didn't leverage any of the skills that I had been developing over the last seven years in the corporate world.

These are a variety of things that I had a great deal of skill in. So as I struggled trying to do the motivational speaking, I didn't make any money doing that. I was forced to go back to my existing skillset and say, how can I make money as the guy who knows tech and software. I started developing websites and doing different technical stuff for customers, because that's where I was able to make money.

That led to all kinds of opportunities, including things that I now do and get paid to do as motivational things that I wanted to do. But I first had to bank on and leverage the skills that I already had. So, when you're just getting started in your business look at all the different skills you have already. It's already going to be tough enough to start a new business as it is, don't start a new business where you have zero skills.

Where are skills right now that you can monetize? Think of how you can translate this to the online world. If you're really good at writing and you have a lot of testimonials and clients that hired you for writing, how can you now monetize your services as a writer? Once you monetize your services as a writer you can start creating products that communicate some of these skills to other aspiring writers. If there are things you're an expert at then you can turn your services into products over time.

That's the biggest thing you need to figure out is if you're going to sell. I see a lot of people that want to get into an online business and just try some Facebook system, a blog and other things. I would suggest that you pick a skill you're really good at and figure out a way to sell that skill to existing companies or existing consumers.

This is a good story. I have a customer who was similar to me, doing sales and a lot of project management in the corporate world. She got out of that and had several different side gigs and was basically trying to start her own online business. She did the exact opposite of what I'm suggesting here. She ignored all the skills from the project management corporate world and started trying to build a list, promoting random affiliate products in the Internet marketing niche.

It was a difficult transition because she didn't have any skills or experience in using these products that she was recommending so she had a hard time building a list because there was a disconnect there. She was basically being a middle-person between buyers and sellers, which is a business. But I looked at what she was doing and realized that she was ignoring all these other skills.

She was an excellent project manager. She was really good at reverse-engineering processes and working with people to optimize what they did in their businesses or lives. I connected her with a bunch of other online entrepreneurs, people like myself who were not running their businesses as effectively as they could have. I suggested that she create a project management service, where she could go in and evaluate people's businesses, who they hired, the projects they were running, the types of products they were creating and the systems they used to deliver those products to clients.

She would sit down and evaluate all these different things and provide a solution or proposal or roadmap in order for them to optimize their business. That is something that I would hire somebody to come in and do because they could make me more money in my business. For her, that's a better way of approaching business, because now she's taking on these skills that she did for a decade. She was really good at it and she'd already been paid well by corporations to do it for them, so why not do that under the umbrella of her own business?

I don't know where she went with that, but I know she got started and it was a much better fit than just randomly pedaling products that had nothing to do with her background. This is a great example of something you need to do as you're starting up your business.

Look at the skills you already have and figure out how to make money with those, whether they're products or services. Usually you'll be selling your time in the beginning, until you get good at what you do and then you can turn that into products later on.

Things To Avoid

Do not to sell things or get involved in projects where you have no skill or experience, because you don't know what you don't know and you're very likely going to make bad decisions. You might learn from these decisions which will have value in the long run, but you don't need to cause yourself any extra pain.

Also, be very careful with whom you partner and associate with. It's very easy to take proposals from people that say, I have this idea, why don't you partner with me and we can try to make it work together. If you already have something you are working on, finish your project first before you start taking on partner projects or work with people, especially if you don't have a good deal of information on their background.

I've seen a lot of people that get involved in these projects that never end up going anywhere or they end up taking on more responsibility than they should have. They carry the project which ends up costing them money in their own business. It's good to partner, just make sure you partner with people you trust and that you understand what your entry and exit criteria are.

Something else you want to avoid is jumping around from one idea to the next. If you followed my first piece of advice, which is taking some existing skills that you're really good at and that you know you can make money on, pick a project to implement those skills and finish the project. Go from start to finish, whether it's launching a product or getting a service up and running. Sell that service and finish the job with your clients. Don't leave half-done Complete everything you finish and try to do a few iterations of it.

The business I'm doing right now BestQualityPLR.com, we started with a couple different products and we made $100 profit in the beginning. That was enough to prove that this thing had legs, so we basically did the same thing. We created products over and over and after 20 to 30 we realized that we had a good business. If we had stopped after 5 or 10 and said hey we've made $1000 let's try something else now, we wouldn't have been able to build a very successful business, which now funds our entire lifestyle.

We've built it into a huge business that both myself and my business partner, not only live off of, but we have a number of employees, We're growing it every year and it all started with a very small project that had a little success and we repeated it, Even though it sometimes felt a little boring or monotonous, over time it became more exciting because we got better. We developed our skills and we honed in on one very specific skillset that we got good at, which allowed us to get creative and build a lot of momentum in order to make more money.

If you're jumping around from one topic to the next or from one project or business to the next, you never allow yourself the time to develop extreme skill, focus and credibility in that one area. Therefore, you want to make sure that you avoid changing your mind all the time. Pick something. Don't keep doing it if it isn't working at all. But even if it's just working a little and you're making some money, do more of it and see if you can increase the amount of money you make each time you do an iteration of it.

Find A Mentor

My parting advice to anyone that's leaving the corporate world and wants to start their own business is to find a mentor. As early as you possibly can, find a mentor, someone you can meet either face-to-face or at the very least on Skype. Find someone that's farther down the road from where you are right now, who you'd like to be like and help them out.

Get involved in some of their projects, do some free work for them or take interest in their business and comment on their Facebook pages and their blogs. Try to get on their radar and get involved in their business or inside of a project inside their business. You'll be surprised at the number of big named entrepreneurs who are still open to taking on people they can mentor or work with if they're getting help for free, while receiving real benefit in their business.

You will gain so much just by being around that person. They won't necessarily teach you step by step but you'll learn through observation and osmosis, seeing what they do, how they behave, how they speak to their clients and how they run their operation or deal with their staff.

It was a big deal for me. As soon as I got my first mentor a few years into running my own business, everything took off and more opportunities were presented. I still had to work hard. I still had to go through hell in some cases and it was difficult, but my mentors... those who I was able to observe, watch and learn from... were monumental.

Learn to keep a rigid schedule for yourself where every day you dedicate some time to self-motivation. Keep feeding your mind positive messages and read books. People get their sources of inspiration from anywhere, but it's not just business. It's not just plugging away, doing your work and grinding it out. Take time every day to feed your mind and get yourself to a place where your self-belief is extremely high no matter what. I don't care how bad things look.

If it looks like everything around you is failing and nothing you touch is right that's fine. Keep yourself in a head space of, I'm going to keep going, I'm determined to make this thing happen no matter what. If you give yourself that fuel every single day it will become a habit and things will eventually start working out. You will have amazing days where you're incredibly excited and inspired and then you can carry those successes forward.

In future days where you may be hitting a wall you can then draw from those successes. So stay motivated and feed your mind. It could be through your mentors, books, watching YouTube or other inspirational videos, listening to audios or whatever. Keep yourself in the game and never give up. Stay persistent and you'll make it happen.

From Investment Banking to Making Videos by Sharyn Sheldon

I never wanted to be an entrepreneur. I never saw myself as running a business or managing other people. In fact, I never thought I had the skills or personality to do it. I'm a bit of an introvert and thought that entrepreneurs were all outgoing, energetic, creative, and bold. I really didn't see myself as any of those things.

The problem is that I didn't like having a boss either.

My plan had always been to do well in school, go off to college, get an M.B.A. and work in the field of international finance. After all, that sounded interesting. I was even good at it.

The problem is that just because you're good at something doesn't mean you are going to enjoy it.

Most people say I don't seem like an introvert at all, and they're surprised that I don't have a lot of confidence in myself. However, to get to where I am today I've had to conquer self-doubt and fears, and I've had to learn to do things that I never wanted to do or thought I was capable of.

But I did them anyway, and in some cases I even found I like them! Who ever thought I'd be making videos? I avoided it like the plague for the longest time, even though people told me it was important. And yet, here I am now, making videos on a regular basis. It turns out that I'm not only good at it, but it's one of my favorite things to do.

My journey from corporate world to online entrepreneur has taken several years and a lot of ups and downs. But, look where I am today. I'm a successful entrepreneur, running my own business and taking care of my children at the same time.

Investment Banking and Instructional Design

The corporate world seems so long ago and far away, and that's just fine with me.

I was never truly a 'corporate' type. In fact, even though I was the 'good little girl' and teacher's pet when I was growing up, authority never sat well with me.

If a rule seemed 'stupid', then I wasn't inclined to follow it. Unfortunately, the corporate world is full of those types of rules.

Here's a case in point. I started out my corporate career, after business school, in an investment bank. High powered, wheeling and dealing, macho atmosphere, expense accounts....the whole shebang. Barring the macho part I could handle most of it, except for the total inefficiency of work. As an associate, there was an unspoken competition to see who could spend the most time working. 100 hours a week to get something done that should only take 20 hours at most? You've got to be kidding me! That was total insanity to me.

On top of that, there was the fact that I just couldn't see myself being able to have a career and a family in that business. I looked at the women who had moved up the ladder at that time. They either didn't have families or were divorced. And if they did have a family, they never saw them. It was going to be one or the other, and that just wasn't acceptable to me.

Needless to say, I got out of there as soon as I saw the opportunity. My husband was offered a job in London, and off we went.

After a couple of missteps and a move back to New York, I landed a completely different type of corporate job, consulting in a field I've always loved at heart - learning.

I had no idea a job like this existed! These were people who described their job as 'delivering learning solutions' for companies. Many were instructional designers, which is a far more interesting way of saying that they designed training programs. But, there was far more to it than just your run-of – the-mill training courses. They were carefully designed and developed to address specific business problems that a company was facing.

For example, if a company was unhappy with the speed at which new salespeople were starting to bring in business, the training and development department might call us in. We'd take a close look at everything they were doing currently with those new recruits, and then we'd identify where there were problems or room for improvement. Often it was a mix of issues that required a 'blended learning solution' for not just the salesforce, but also the managers.

You can see how the solutions could get complex very quickly. A blended learning solution could involve everything from your standard classroom course to self-study, virtual webinars, mentoring arrangements, resource websites and more.

It was fascinating work and I had to learn everything on the job. So much for my fancy M.B.A., though it certainly gave me some credibility in corporate eyes.

Corporate America Exodus

There are basically 3 types of people who leave corporate America. The first are people who get fired and can't find another job, or decide at that point it's a good time to make a change. They have no choice in the matter. The second are people who make the decision to chuck it all in, quit the J.O.B. and strike out on their own - with or without a plan. I don't recommend that unless you have plenty of funds in place.

Then there are people like me, for whom it's a gradual process, born from a mix of circumstance, need, and desire.

The first step was when my daughter was born and I managed to get my employer to agree to let me work at least 1 day a week from home. That gave me the first real taste of freedom. Then, along came the twins. Desire became desperation, and I needed a lot more flexibility. With one two year old and two baby boys, there was no way I was going to be handing them off to a nanny and heading to work. Luckily, my company had a "resource network" of consultants that they hired on a project by project basis. It was the perfect solution for me.

That situation morphed into working as a consultant with a couple of former colleagues, in an informal arrangement. I pretty much relied on one of my consultant friends for work, since she was a terrific salesperson and able to easily bring in clients. Never in my most vivid nightmares did I imagine myself "selling" and trying to sign up clients on my own. I had enough to handle with 3 little children.

At that point, I was still working with corporations, so I definitely don't consider that leaving corporate America. As long as your work is at the mercy of bureaucracy and the whims of the latest economic or management change, you're corporate.

Fast forward to 9/11 and my whole perspective started to change. I was working across the street from the World Trade Center for a client when the towers were hit. After fleeing up the West Side Highway and finally making it home later that afternoon, I knew life was going to change for me – one way or another.

Business after that was so up and down that I never knew when I would have paid work. My main client moved all their operations away from the World Trade Center area to a location about 2 ½ hours away from me. That meant that every meeting required most of the day driving and the usual child care nightmares that anyone working full time has.

To top it off, I was still reliant on my colleague for any projects. It was ok for the time being, since I wanted to be there for my children as much as possible. However, looking ahead, I really couldn't see myself doing the same work long term. It had become too rote and boring. All my income was completely dependent on someone else's decisions, so I was just biding my time until I could figure something out. I was grateful for whatever work I could get, but it wasn't something I looked forward to.

During one of those down times, when I didn't have any work and was stressing about the future, my husband gave me the idea of working online. He said, "how about starting a content website? You're a good writer and I hear that's a great way to make money." Sounded good to me. Unfortunately, we had no idea what that involved.

But off I headed anyway. I cut the cord on a business I really wasn't enthusiastic about anyway and dove into a world I knew absolutely nothing about.

Leaving Without Research and Planning

I never really "prepared" for leaving the corporate world, unless you can call working as an independent consultant preparation. You could say that knowing how to work from home and manage my own time was probably the best preparation I could have.

However, the part that didn't happen, that everyone leaving corporate should do, is the research and planning stage. I jumped into something that sounded like a good idea and fun without spending the time to research different business models and deciding on what would make most sense for me.

The result was that I floundered for a while in areas where I learned a lot, like building little niche marketing websites, but which didn't really suit my skills and personality.

I even spent a full year redesigning and building up a wedding favors website that looks amazing. Just don't ask me how much traffic it gets or income. It's too embarrassing!

When it came down to finding the right business to build, I ended up going back to my roots in instructional design. Just because I didn't enjoy it in the corporate world didn't mean I had to abandon my skills completely. I simply had to apply them to a new market who valued what I had to offer.

Private Label Rights

The online business I eventually discovered and built was one I'd never heard of before. Private Label Rights or PLR for short. PLR typically consists of some type of digital content that people can buy, customize, and then put their own name on. The benefit for the buyers is that they don't have to create their content from scratch. The bulk of the research and creation has been done for them.

PLR can be compared to white label products in the offline world. Think about that can of peas with the supermarket brand label on it. The supermarkets probably didn't make those themselves. Instead, they bought a white label version and put their own label on. You can find white label cosmetics, food, direct marketing materials, drugs, clothing etc.

My own online business, which I called Business Content PLR, started out as focusing on business-related, digital content. From the start, I differentiated myself by bringing in my instructional design background and giving everything a learning focus. Instead of the traditional packs of articles that many PLR sellers offered, I added worksheets, checklists, templates and other material that would help people implement what they learned.

Since then, I've started producing what I call "white label training programs". These are very similar to the types of training programs I created for corporations, but anyone can buy and use them as if they'd designed them for themselves. And of course, they're a LOT cheaper.

Now business coaches, trainers, service providers, or anyone wanting to teach a course can just buy one of mine. Then they can customize it to their own needs and be off and running. They're what I like to call "express training solutions".

People love them! Who would have guessed that I'd hear such great feedback for something I did on a regular basis in my corporate projects? You don't get people writing to you with praise and thanks when you're in corporate America. Well, maybe some people do, but it didn't happen to me until I left that world behind entirely.

Challenges To Leaving The Corporate World

For anyone thinking about leaving the corporate world, there are a few big obstacles that you're going to have to face.

The first is timing. You'll have to think about when you'll leave, whether it will be sudden or gradual, how much time you really want to spend, etc. Take a careful look at your finances before you make any sudden moves. How long can you survive on your current savings?

No matter what some people say, it can take months or even years to build up to the same level of income you currently have. If you can't afford to be without an income for long, you're best off if you start a business on the side and build it up gradually in your spare time.

The second HUGE challenge you'll face is deciding what you want to do. You'll hear a plethora of ideas, advice, 'guaranteed' systems, and other supposedly easy money solutions. Listen, but not too hard.

There are a lot of opportunities out there, but not all of them are right for you. Good research and self-analysis can help you figure out the right one. Take a look at what the main business models are and think about where your own skills and personality fit best. You could start an offline retail business or sell physical products online. You could sell your expert services as an independent consultant or service provider, such as a writer, virtual assistant or business coach. And of course, you could start an internet-based business, selling your own or other people's products. Spend some time on the internet researching different models and their potential. Then go with what makes most sense to you.

As a little side note, remember that just because a business looks great to you doesn't mean it will be successful. You'll need to find a business model you like, and then you'll need to figure out your target market. I can't go into all the details of target marketing here, but that's one thing you MUST learn

The third challenge is self-management. The best thing about being in a corporate environment is that you tend to have structured hours and clear responsibilities. Once you leave that world, you have to create your own structure.

The time management challenge is the reason there are so many books out there on this very topic. You'll find all sorts of software, systems and processes for effective time management. I got used to tracking my time when I was a consultant since we charged clients based on the hours we spent. We also estimated the cost of projects based on how long we forecast it would take. That habit has always served me well.

I highly recommend scheduling your work time for specific slots during the day or night, depending on your own commitments and when you focus best. Keep track of it with whatever tool you like. Make daily to-do lists that are short and longer to-do lists for the week or month. Learn what tasks take you longer and look for ways to shorten that time. It takes some practice, but managing your time is critical. It's all too easy to let your own business seep into every corner of your life when it's not restricted to a 9 to 5 schedule.

First Step – Research, Research, Research

Research, research, research. If there's one thing that can absolutely determine your failure as an entrepreneur, it's lack of research.

Just as you needed to do research to figure out your best business model, it's equally important to examine your target customers and the competition you'll face. Jumping into a market with only a gut instinct, hope, and prayer might result in huge success or dismal financial disaster.

Take the time to analyze your target market, communicate with them, look for opportunities, and actually test out your ideas before you commit. You'll save yourself time and money in the long run because you'll be putting effort into a business that you already know can succeed.

Focus. The next biggest indicator of success (or failure) is being able to focus on your core business and marketing strategy. The online world is extremely distracting for any business – online or offline. Spending time on Facebook and Twitter might be an important part of some businesses' marketing plan, but it isn't necessarily for you.

You'll be inundated all the time with ideas for other business enterprises or ways to make easy money. Sure, those businesses might earn you additional income, but they'll also take away from the one you're trying to build. When you spend a little amount of time on 5 different enterprises, it will take you 5 times as long to make any of them succeed. Instead, focus on building up one and then outsourcing or automating as much as possible before starting another.

Network. I thought moving to working online would mean I wouldn't have to deal with people much. I was so wrong! You need to get out there and meet people, whether it's face to face or virtually. That's how you'll get answers to your questions, introductions to potential customers, advice for moving your business ahead, and a little social interaction too. Things can get lonely when you're working out of your house and rarely seeing real people.

Face-to-face networking can involve going to conferences, local meetups, special networking hours, and even community events. Virtual networking can be just as effective. Facebook Groups, special forums in your market, or paid coaching membership sites can all be great places to meet like-minded people. Take the attitude of helping others first, and then they'll be there to help you when you need it.

Avoid The "Easy Button"

The biggest thing you need to avoid is the 'easy button'. It's so tempting when you see people offering a quick, proven way to make money. Listen a little, if it's someone you already trust. Otherwise, run away!

The old saying still holds. If something looks too good to be true, then it probably isn't true.

Parting Advice

When I first made the decision to start an online business, one of my good friends told me "If you don't have a Plan B, then you have to make Plan A work." That philosophy, and a good dose of stubbornness, has kept me going over and over, even when it seemed I'd never build my business enough to be profitable. If you truly want to get out of the corporate world, then going back can't be an option in your mind.

My other advice is to get a coach when you get stuck. It doesn't have to be right at the start, but get it in your head now that you'll need to enlist some paid advice at some point. Each time I've hired someone to get me through a tough time, it's paid off. It often takes someone with a different perspective to help you see where you need to make little changes that can grow your business to a new level.

Sharyn Sheldon is a solopreneur who has built a successful online business selling white label training programs for business coaches, trainers and service providers. Her customizable, ready-to-go content saves her customers tremendous amounts of time so that they can focus on what they do best – serve their own clients and build their own businesses.

You can find Sharyn at BusinessContentPLR.com. Otherwise, she's out with her husband and three children, reading a good mystery novel, or doing some Zumba.

Conclusion

I hope after reading everyone's online marketing journey that you feel inspired to get started right away. As you can see everyone's journey is a little different. We all started from different places but in the end, we all have an online marketing business. The whole point of this book was to encourage your entrepreneurial spirit and give you the courage to start now. Hopefully something someone said has sparked an "I can do this too" mindset.

In order to be a successful online marketer, you have to have the proper mindset, a strong reason why and a step-by-step plan for starting your business. Mindset has a lot to do with being successful in any endeavor including online marketing. There are a couple of Kindle books that I recommend that show you the right mental attitude you must possess to be successful. Anthony Robbins' Awaken the Giant Within (http://amzn.to/1r3BZVU) is a great book that teaches you strategies for mastering your emotions, relationships, finances and your life in general. There is also a great book about mindset that is related specifically to online and internet marketing. The Inner Game of Internet Marketing (http://amzn.to/1sup9Oy) by Connie Ragen Green and Geoff Hoff teaches you how to successfully navigate the waters of online marketing as an entrepreneur.

Starting an online marketing business is hard work but it is very fulfilling in the end. You need to have a strong reason why to sustain you during the tough times. Most online marketers have many more reasons than money for wanting to be an entrepreneur. What Is You Why (http://amzn.to/1reTWT2) is a book where students of Connie Ragen Green explain why they are pursuing an online marketing business.

If you still have a full-time job, then more than likely you will start you online marketing business on a part-time basis first. There are two books that teach you how to make the transition from a job to an online marketer. The Weekend Marketer (http://amzn.to/1uK7FBl) by Connie Ragen Green teaches you have to say goodbye to the "9 to 5" and build an online business. Click Millionaires (http://amzn.to/1tnhtSa) by Scott Fox teaches you how to trade the 9-5 job you hate for an online business

If you would to learn how to create your own compilation Kindle book, then you can download an audio and study guide that teaches you step-by-step how to do this yourself. To get started today with creating your first Kindle book, visit Create Your Compilation Book:
(http://createmycompilationbook.com/).

If you would like more information about Leave The Corporate Word Behind and how to start an online marketing business, please visit our website,
www.leavethecorporateworldbehind.com.

www.ingramcontent.com/pod-product-compliance
Lightning Source LLC
Chambersburg PA
CBHW070931210326
41520CB00021B/6886